The Disabled God Revisited

The Disabled God Revisited

Trinity, Christology, and Liberation

Lisa D. Powell

t&tclark

LONDON • NEW YORK • OXFORD • NEW DELHI • SYDNEY

T&T CLARK
Bloomsbury Publishing Plc
50 Bedford Square, London, WC1B 3DP, UK
1385 Broadway, New York, NY 10018, USA
29 Earlsfort Terrace, Dublin 2, Ireland

BLOOMSBURY, T&T CLARK and the T&T Clark logo are trademarks of
Bloomsbury Publishing Plc

First published in Great Britain 2023

A catalogue record for this book is available from the British Library.

A catalog record for this book is available from the Library of Congress.

ISBN: HB: 978-0-5676-9434-8
PB: 978-0-5676-9433-1
ePDF: 978-0-5676-9436-2
ePUB: 978-0-5676-9435-5

Typeset by Newgen KnowledgeWorks Pvt. Ltd., Chennai, India

To find out more about our authors and books visit www.bloomsbury.com
and sign up for our newsletters.

For the Marys:
Mary Corinne
Mary Ellen
Mary Ruth
and their namesake:
Marigold Inez

CONTENTS

ACKNOWLEDGMENTS

Often in the past few years, while teaching during Covid-19 and parenting young children who learned from home for much of a year, I've thought perhaps I should be content with a few articles out of this research and be done. But I've motivated myself by thinking about this section of the book and telling myself I have to finish so I can publicly and more permanently thank these people, especially "the Marys" to whom this book is dedicated. So bear with me in this extended tale of all the help required to bring this project to fruition. I'm nothing if not sentimental.

I started the research for this book on semester sabbatical in the spring of 2017 when our son Walden was one and daughter Marigold was three. Those familiar with the cost of childcare, especially for young children, understand our struggle to find full-time childcare we could afford that could support the kind of work desired and expected of a sabbatical. We cobbled time together somehow between the Marys and briefly using a part-time church daycare that closed down less than three months after it opened. My husband, John, had just graduated and was in his first semester teaching high school biology, so his days were full. I would drop the kids off with John's mom, Mary Ellen, or with our kids' adopted grandma, Mary Corinne, and typically then call my mother, Mary Ruth, as I drove to the room lent to me by the Sisters of Humility in Davenport, Iowa. There I would read blissfully for hours on end, lunch with the accomplished and fascinating women of the order, and be overcome with gratitude for the people in my life making this possible. I'm thankful that the Sisters so generously offered me this space and shared their meals and lives with me.

Our family's reliance on the Marys was nothing new. As my husband had been in school full time since our daughter was an infant, we had depended on them to fill many gaps in our days. For hours each week they played, read, snuggled, and loved our children so we could pursue research, work, and study. This book is dedicated to them because we couldn't have done our work well or with the peace with which we were able, without their loving presence and commitment to supporting us and our family.

As will be clear in the reading of this book, not only are these ideas inspired by the contributions of Nancy Eiesland to liberation theology, they are also (surprisingly even to me) deeply indebted to the work of systematic theologian Bruce McCormack. To be honest, I never expected to engage McCormack's work, and had been largely ignorant of his corpus while a student at Princeton Theological Seminary (PTS). Most people who do their PhDs in systematic theology at PTS go there to study Barth (though obviously not all) and would then certainly be familiar with Bruce's influence in Barth studies. My relationship with Bruce was different because it related to our upbringing in the Church of the Nazarene. As an MDiv student deeply shaped by the Wesleyan Holiness tradition, I was often perplexed by my peers at the Presbyterian school. I felt out of place, like students and faculty didn't understand my language, and to some extent my faith, because I was on such a passionate quest for holiness. Bruce taught me an independent study course on Wesley's theology and met with me many times over lunch in the dining room on campus. I shared freely with him about how spiritually weary I was on this pursuit of Christian Perfection familiar to those from my tradition; he assured me of God's acceptance of me, and I know he was praying for me. And although I didn't work with Bruce much for my PhD, years later his description of the origin of God's triunity drove home an understanding of God's commitment to us in a way that, I think, helps me love God more, which is one of the reasons I wrote this book. I hope that translating the dense systematic work of McCormack and others into the language of liberation theology, and (hopefully) into a more accessible vocabulary, this book will likewise help others see the depths of God's commitment to us and this world.

This book is inspired by a fierce belief in God's faithfulness and grace that grew through my studies and relationships at PTS. I consider this a gift I received from the Reformed tradition and from many friends and colleagues shaped by it, especially Erin Kesterson Bowers who once said to me: "See, you sing songs about how you have decided to follow Jesus, but we'd never sing that, because God has decided." There is an assurance and a rest in that affirmation that my spirit has finally been granted. PTS also brought a number of other people into my life who continue to be important for my theological and personal development: I'm grateful especially to Alice

Yafeh and Sarah Zhang for celebrating even small accomplishments and for their monthly check-ins on life and research goals, and to Jen Bayne, a constant support and committed friend, who screams "Maranatha" with me against the void.

When I presented some of the material found in Chapter 5 of this book at the Annual Meeting of the Society of Christian Ethics someone at the session asked me if I've seen examples of the sort of Care Webs I describe at the end of the paper. I said the closest thing I'd encountered was the St. Paul Mom's Facebook Group, where meal trains are created for people who are sick or who've just had a baby, and where calls for diapers are met with boxes stacked to the ceiling. Our family is indebted to the community at St. Paul Lutheran Church. When my husband, Marigold, and I had Covid-19 at the same time this summer, we had multiple offers for groceries and meals. This church gave us our Covid pod, our camping crew, and an extended family of extra grown-ups to care for our children, and kids who are like cousins to our own. Justine, Sara (Red Hot), and Sara (Hot Sauce) encouraged me when I despaired, fixed us meals, hosted play dates, and made me laugh throughout this journey; I am grateful.

St. Ambrose University (SAU) has also been supportive of my work, and I am thankful to be able to study and teach theology in a place that embraces justice at the heart of its mission. I'm grateful for the support of the Dean of the College of Arts and Sciences, Pat Archer, who invited me to present this research at the Liberal Arts Lecture, and for my colleagues who, despite knowing little about theology, showed up with interest anyway. The Baecke Endowment for the Humanities funded my participation in the Barth Center's Conference on Barth and Liberation Theology in 2018, where I was able to present some preliminary research and get helpful feedback from fellow scholars. Many colleagues in the theology department have been sources of encouragement and valuable sounding boards for this work especially Mara Adams, Bud Grant, and Tadd Ruetenik in Philosophy. Professor Emeritus (Mary) Corinne Winter read the entire manuscript and gave me crucial feedback. I owe special thanks to Joyce Haack in the library who tracked down countless articles and books for me through interlibrary loan, too often on short notice and sometimes not without great effort; she has been an amazing help! I also want to recognize the students at SAU who energize me in their passion for justice, especially those who took liberation theology in the fall of 2021. Isabelle, Laura, Samantha, and the rest of the class, dug into hard texts, asked great questions, and remind me of my deep love for this work. Thanks also to the women of Triota for helping me find my activist feet again.

During the initial Covid-19 shut down, an interdisciplinary network of support emerged among some of my colleagues at SAU. This beautiful band of creative scholars and artists, the Rebel Studies Department, offered fortitude with care packages, virtual quarantinis, Schitt's Creek memes, and perpetual chat. They continue to foster friendship, humor, and wisdom. Thank you, Rebels.

I'm not sure this book would have been written if Anna Turton at T&T Clark didn't send me an email when we were at a small conference together and ask if I would speak with her about my teaching and research in liberation theology. I was impressed that she is seeking out scholars with no name recognition and topics sometimes spurned in systematic theology. How else will we gather more voices to the table if publishers aren't actively reaching out to gather contributions from scholars not already piled into bibliographies and citations? Hopefully my citations will help push the work of disability scholars into the minds and libraries of more systematicians.

When I started graduate school I was a bit obsessed with the film *Yentl*, where Barbara Streisand's character dresses to pass as a man so that she can study the Talmud. Disguised as a man she marries a woman, who then brings her snacks and tea while she studies and reads. I dreamed of such a life: hours on end reading and thinking without having to stop to get up for tea or crackers. I've had the joy of many such moments thanks to my partner, John Arnold. He went back to school when Marigold was born so that we could have similar schedules to maximize time as a family. As I've worked on this book the past two summers, he's taken the kids on extra camping trips and bike rides, to swimming holes and museums. He's built dozens of Lego forts and whittled arrows and walking sticks. He knew what I needed and wanted was time, and he gave that to me, and also packed me lunches and brewed me tea. I couldn't have finished this without him.

Marigold wants to be a writer someday, probably of books about dragons, but she's championed me in the writing of this less fantastical text nonetheless, and Walden has insisted on giving me daily snuggles and butterfly kisses, and I have needed every single one of them. All together they've offered me an abundance of affection and love. The kids cheered when I told them I'd sent this manuscript in.

Perhaps the most important thing I've learned since beginning this book in 2017 relates to Eva Kittay's line: "A truly independent life—one in which we need no one—would be a very impoverished one, even if it were possible."[1] I've needed a lot of people in life, of course, and I've relied on many just to get this slim volume to print. I wouldn't want it any other way; this entangled and needy life is a glimpse of heaven, and "my cup runneth over."

[1] Eva Kittay, *Learning from My Daughter: The Value and Care of Disabled Minds* (Oxford: Oxford University Press, 2019), 161.

Introduction

A Confession

A confession is warranted: I am not currently disabled, although chronic illness played a significant part in my childhood and adolescence. I also know that at any moment my physical, cognitive, and mental status may change. And although I am the parent of a neurodivergent child, I am writing, in effect, as an outsider. I receive the social and structural benefits of being non-disabled and being perceived as such. Nevertheless, disability theory and theology, have been vital to my formation as a liberation theologian. The critiques that disability studies bring to feminist theory and theology, for example, expose ways in which even the best-intentioned ideas can replicate social values that denigrate the lives of others. Disability is a crucial perspective in liberation theology. It crosses every context with the force of intersectionality. For example, people with disabilties are twice as likely to be poor in the United States, and people of color are disproportionately disabled. People with disabilities constitute the largest "minority" population, and most people are impacted by disability at some point in their lives: through a parent who becomes physically or mentally impaired as they grow older, a sibling in the home with a mental illness or physical impairment, or one's own temporary or enduring disability acquired at birth or through an accident, illness, or aging. And yet disability is the most overlooked perspective in our liberationist conversations, where we repeatedly critique the assumption of normativity given to the white cis-gendered, heterosexual male, but we rarely remember that this norm is also an able-bodied one.

I've taught sections of Nancy Eiesland's book *The Disabled God: Toward a Liberatory Theology of Disability* for more than ten years to undergraduates.[1] Occasionally we read the whole book, but more often students read her chapter on Eucharist in a course introducing the basics of Christian doctrine. Whereas students typically have a spiritualized and almost magical association with communion, if they have any ideas about it at all, Eiesland's focus on the physical nature of the sacrament is fresh to them. Eiesland, as a disability theologian, emphasizes the bodily nature of communion, both our own physical participation in the rite, taking the bread and eating, sometimes processing and kneeling, and also the reality of the body we receive: Jesus' broken body. This sacrament is central to the gathering of the body of Christ that is the church, which she calls a "communion of struggle." Her indictment of exclusionary practices around this sacrament are important, and my students sometimes react strongly against her criticism of certain ways of administering this sacrament that may encourage people with certain disabilities to remain in their seats instead of partaking with the rest of the congregation at the front of the church where there are too often steps up to the altar and an expectation of kneeling. The Eucharist as a sacrament around which the body of Christ gathers, remembers the perpetually broken and impaired body of Jesus; he remains disabled. This practice supports her claim that impaired bodies are perfectly acceptable to God and welcomed into the resurrected life without need of a fix or cure, as Jesus' wounds were resurrected with his body and returned to God. This claim of impaired bodies in heaven is one of her most contested—challenged by my students, numerous theologians, and people with disabilities. I will address that claim in the final chapter of this book, but to get there, I will first attend to her claim that God is disabled because of Jesus' wounded body, a claim that is less developed in her book, but foundational to her argument.

Trinity, Christology, and Liberation Theology

The idea for this book began when I read an article related to a fierce debate raging in Barth studies over the logical priority of election

---

[1]Nancy Eiesland, *The Disabled God: Toward a Liberatory Theology of Disability* (Nashville, TN: Abingdon Press, 1994).

to triunity. One proposal caught my attention because it resonated with the picture of God shaped for me by liberation theologies, including that of Eiesland. Here was a God who takes embodiment seriously, who embraces creaturely life with a depth reaching into the very being of Godself, and who truly identifies with the entire life, ministry, and suffering of Jesus, such that the Son is eternally shaped to be this specific person. Frankly, I was surprised to find myself so drawn to an account of God coming from Barth studies.

I am not a Barth scholar, but I completed my PhD at Princeton Theological Seminary in Systematic Theology, where I was surrounded by them. Course work in the program was difficult, not because it was challenging and rigorous, though of course it was that. But because of the way theology was typically debated in seminars by male classmates there to study Barth, occasionally encouraged in this behavior by certain faculty members. Other women in the program and I often felt silenced, talked over, and diminished. The whole Barthian scene felt like a manifestation of masculinist hegemony, stifling to this Wesleyan woman with an emerging commitment to liberation theology. So I never expected to return to Barth after I completed my requirements there, and certainly never expected to devote myself to a controversy in Barth studies that has been combative and vitriolic in many ways.

I came across the debate because a friend and colleague got mixed up in it all, and I was curious. So I read Bruce McCormack's "Seek God Where He May Be Found," as well as a series of articles written in response.[2] I was shocked to find myself moved by the account of God outlined in McCormack's article and sought out more, including the essay that ignited the controversy: "Grace and Being: The Role of God's Gracious Election in Karl Barth's Theological Ontology."[3] I did not care in the least which was the "truer" reading of Barth, or whether or not a significant shift in Barth's thought was demonstrable, as some claimed. I simply found that McCormack's position articulated an understanding of God that somehow cohered with the liberation theologies that had

---

[2]Bruce McCormack, "Seek God Where He May Be Found: A Response to Edwin van Driel," *Scottish Journal of Theology* 60 (1) (2007): 62–79.
[3]Bruce McCormack, "Grace and Being: The Role of God's Gracious Election in Karl Barth's Theological Ontology," in *The Cambridge Companion to Karl Barth*, ed. John Webster (Cambridge: Cambridge University Press, 2000), 92–110.

rescued my faith years ago, while offering a precision of doctrinal explication for which I longed.

This book will, in part, develop some of the promise that I see in this conception of God for the concerns of liberation theology, particularly disability theology as introduced in Nancy Eiesland's *The Disabled God*. But how, you may ask, could debates about the primordial ordering of the being of God have bearing on the pressing concerns of the oppressed in our world? Or you may resonate with Ivone Gebara's summary of common lack of interest in the Trinity: "It seems to take place far from us, far from our own flesh and concerns. And besides, it seems to be a sharing among 'persons' who are totally spiritual and perfect. It is, after all, a divine communion that barely affects us."[4] In fairness there is no policy proposal or action plan for social change in this book. However, liberation theologians have long asserted that our God-talk matters, and there is here a proposal for the origin of God's triunity that helps one to understand more fully that the divine life is neither "far off from our own flesh" nor "totally spiritual." It is an understanding of the shape of God's life that demonstrates the remarkable depth of God's solidarity with creation, with the marginalized, and with the disabled.

Sketch of the Book

Many texts in disability theology offer a survey of the literature and the development of disability studies and its impact on theological discourse in recent years. I do not retrace that work in this book. Instead I focus primarily on Eiesland's contribution as I endeavor specifically to offer more theological ground to the vision of God she sketches in her book. In Chapter 1, "Nancy Eiesland and the *Disabled God*," I place Eiesland's groundbreaking book in the context of the emerging discipline of disability studies and the movement for disability rights. I summarize her theological contributions, particularly those claims that will be fundamental to the argument of this book. I also engage the criticisms of her argument, giving special attention to the critiques of John

---

[4]Ivone Gebara, *Longing for Running Water: Ecofeminism and Liberation* (Minneapolis, MN: Fortress, 1999), 138.

Swinton in his influential and oft cited article "Who Is the God We Worship."[5]

In Chapter 2, "Covenant Ontology and the Impaired Body of the Son," I explain the proposal for the triune life of God as shaped for covenant relationship, such that the very nature of God as triune may be considered a result of God's self-determination to be a God of covenant relationship outside Godself. Here the argument is quite technical, pertaining to theological ontology, or the nature of God's being, and particularly protology or the way we can think of the origin of God's being, that is the "beginning" for the One who is eternal and thus has no true "beginning." The argument relies on the belief that who God is revealed to be in the economy of salvation (that is the way God engages with creation in time and history through Jesus and the Spirit) truly is who God is within Godself (or in the immanent Trinity). The boldness of this reading of the revelation of the triune life through the life and ministry of Jesus and his reliance on the Spirit is contested, and I will address some of those critiques in Chapters 3 and 4.

Chapter 2 is where I make the most obvious advances in Eiesland's argument that God is disabled. Whereas she argued that God is disabled because Jesus, as God incarnate, resurrected and returned to God as one with impairment (by retaining the wounds inflicted in his crucifixion), I will argue even further that God the Son is eternally shaped for this humanity and embodiment, including Jesus' broken body. Based on the covenant ontology proposed we identify no Son other than the one eternally determined to be incarnate in broken flesh, and we can affirm that God as Son truly experiences embodied life, including the suffering associated with it.

However, I ultimately don't want to base the argument for the disabled God, as Eiesland does, on the wounds of Jesus' crucifixion. The tradition, with few exceptions, associates the cross as the punishment for sin, so founding the claim of God's disablement solely in this event of torture and death may risk reinscribing an association of impairment with sin, suffering, and death, which Eiesland certainly didn't want to do, as part of her book specifically critiques that linkage. She highlights the ordinary lives

---

[5]John Swinton, "Who Is the God We Worship? Theologies of Disability; Challenges and New Possibilities," *International Journal of Practical Theology* 14 (2) (2011): 273–307.

of people with disabilities, of people's hopes, desires, loves, and losses common to most humanity. She, along with other disability theologians, seeks to break the association of disability with sin. And so I push beyond the disability that could be identified with Jesus' resurrected body and consider the ways in which God may be considered dependent or in need, which is also a central theme in Eiesland's book.

In Chapter 3, "The Vulnerability and Need of God," I explore the Christological implications for the ontology laid out in Chapter 2 by way of a kenotic Christology that reads the abasement associated with the incarnation as the addition of humanity rather than as a divestment of divine attributes. I do not provide a detailed history of the Christological debates behind the question of how the divine and human natures in Christ exist in the one person of Jesus, nor do I detail the differing nuances of various kenotic Christologies and their history. Excellent research by historians of doctrine have done this work. Instead, drawing from the work of Bruce McCormack, I devote the chapter to considering the Son as ontologically receptive, as one constituted for receiving the humanity of Jesus, and I tease out some of the implications of this receptivity for disability theology.

This understanding of the identity of the Son, however, is related to Karl Barth's conception of the eternally obedient nature of the Son, which is highly criticized for its apparent divinization of hierarchy. A theologian committed to the liberation and flourishing of all of God's creation (which I hope I am) would not be able to accept a hierarchy as divinely ordained, nor affirm Barth's attempts to link the obedience of the Son to the Father with a subordination of women to men. Just as easily as a theology can locate a gender hierarchy in the divine order of God, which is correlated with heteronormativity, so too can one suppose a hierarchy of being with the nondisabled body-mind elevated above the body-mind of those with disabilities. Thus, in Chapter 4 I give special attention to the critiques of Barth's analogy of relation, or the way in which he claims the obedience of the Son is analogous to the rightful subordination of women.

Here I engage theologians who identify an emphasis on the order of the processions of the triune "persons" as the locus of the hierarchical rendering of triune life and justification of social hierarchy. I propose that covenant ontology disallows an account of trinitarian distinctions founded in order because the distinct missions of the trinitarian persons precedes the order of processions. God is determined "first" for covenant, and the processions are directed toward that aim and are not independent of it. God's being is utterly determined for loving communion with creation, and not initially solely for intra-trinitarian communion. I conclude by modestly proposing a structure of call–response to replace the command–obey binary of Barth's theology.

The Christology proposed here finds ontological need in the being of God, as the Son's identity cannot be fulfilled or complete without the incarnation, without real human existence integral to the Son's personhood. Not only does God need creation as that to which God may enter into covenant relationship, but further the Son relies upon the Spirit to guide the action and real decision-making of the humanity of Jesus. God risks Godself from eternity in God's decision to be determined for covenant.

In Chapter 4, "The Receptivity of God," I follow Eiesland's claim that God experiences ontological need, and further the conversation around the receptivity of the Son. I engage some concerns from within liberation theology, especially feminist and queer theology, with notions of kenosis and vulnerability. Receptivity has traditionally been associated with female physiology, subordinated to an assumed male initiative and agency. Women are likewise simultaneously cast as vulnerable and unable to provide for themselves, or "needing a man," and society functions so as to keep women vulnerable economically and physically. Thus, some feminists are rightfully concerned about the impact of elevating vulnerability as a value when social forces and institutions are structured to keep women in deleterious states of dependency and vulnerability.

Yet, feminist disability studies has criticized much modern feminism for its acceptance of the modern liberal value of independence; feminist discourse has too often sought space for women within a social structure that denigrates the lives of those with disabilities. Feminist theory that projects the image of women as utterly without need of assistance, alongside men who are also independent, push women with disabilities (and all in need of care) outside their image of responsible citizens and worthy examples of women's achievement. Feminist discourse must have room for those who are weak, chronically ill, developmentally impaired, or in need of care.

I engage the work of queer systematic theologian Linn Tonstad on the notion of receptivity in trinitarian theology and Christology. Tonstad is highly critical of theologies that rely upon one making room for the other, or receptivity that could be perceived as penetrability, and she traces a heteronormative function through multiple theologies that work within such a frame. Though appreciative of Tonstad's careful analysis of the misogyny and heterosexism behind some of the most influential theologies of the twentieth and twenty-first centuries, I challenge her assumption that receptivity need be figured as a particularly feminine trait. While I certainly agree that receptivity has been figured as feminine historically, I argue that such associations must be challenged head on. Women are not singularly receptive, and receptivity itself need not be feared as inevitably lacking in agency or will. We should not accept a valuation of receptivity as necessarily subordinate to an assumed penetration.

While honoring Tonstad's concerns about heteronormativity in theology, I draw from Crip theorists around sexuality to include the voices of those with disabilities to the critique of doctrines of God and Christ that marginalize those who defy the heteroableist constructions of normativity that are buttressed in these doctrines. People with disabilities are especially targeted in their sexuality, and more scholars and activists are pointing to this aspect of life as a particular place of pernicious attacks on the humanity of people with disabilities. Yet it gets little attention in disability theology and is rarely, if ever, included in queer theology, even though many in the disability community identify as queer, or more than one-third of people in the LGBTQ community identify as disabled.

People with disabilities are likely to engage in sexual intimacy in ways that are different from the normative, procreative, male–female coitus of Christian culture that also serves as analogy for various theological relations. Any critique of the heteronormative and patriarchal rendering of these relations need also consider how people with disabilities are impacted by this ubiquitous analogy of procreative coupling. Thus, as I consider the ontological receptivity of the Son I challenge the gendered association of receptivity and seek to disentangle the sexed associations of giving and receiving, penetration and receptivity, and look at ways in which the being of God and Christ calls us to transvaluate positions of need, receptivity, and vulnerability. I offer two examples to reconceive the alternative power and agency in receptivity. One example comes from queer, trans theological ethicist Roberto Che Espinoza on the power generated in the margins of the margins. The other comes from feminist philosopher Eva Kittay on the agency of those who are receptive of care.

Chapter 5, "Disability and Resurrection," deals with what may be Eiesland's most discussed and lasting claim in *The Disabled God:* that disabilities will be retained in the resurrected life because Jesus was resurrected with his wounds. I survey some of the historical material around impairment in the resurrected body to highlight the ways in which cultural ideals about beauty are reflected in the theological speculations around embodiment in the resurrected life in order to challenge the assumption that resurrected bodies will cohere with sociocultural assumptions about beauty.

Ultimately I question Eiesland's claim that "disabled" bodies are retained in the resurrected life, not because all bodies become perfectly symmetrical, "beautiful," and athletically able-bodied, but because I deny that the category of "disabled" remains. I contend that the binary opposition of disabled–abled will no longer exist, and thus the identity category of "disabled" as it is shaped by an ableist society will no longer be meaningful. In this chapter, I engage liberation theologies that refuse to utilize identity categories created by white supremacist, ableist, heteropatriarchal structures. They challenge the liberative potential that can be harnessed in categories created for the economic and political exploitation of those consigned to subordinated groups.

I argue for an understanding of the resurrected life that includes ongoing transformation as we become increasingly incorporated into the body of Christ, where we receive our identities. His person has already been understood to be dependent and receptive, and so the resurrected life can be understood as one in which we become more like Christ in our interdependence, purified of any lingering sense of independence, truly shaped by and for communal life. Ability ceases to be a category and so "disability" has no functional purpose other than a way to indicate the interconnectedness of all of life in God.

1

Nancy Eiesland and
The Disabled God

Introduction

Disability studies as an academic discipline in the United States
sprang from the disability rights movement and activism of the
1960s and 1970s, which achieved a series of advances in legislation,
including the Architectural Barriers Act of 1968, the Rehabilitation
Act of 1973, and the Education for All Handicapped Children Act
of 1975. Likely the most well-known text of disability theology dates
early to the rise of disability studies: Nancy Eiesland's *The Disabled
God: Toward a Liberatory Theology of Disability*, published in
1994 in the wake of the victory of the Americans with Disabilities
Act achieved in 1990.[1]

Eiesland's work situated disability theology in the stream of
liberation theologies expanding in the 1980s and 1990s, and her work
relied upon similar sociological methodologies, utilizing minority
group theory and stigma theory to advance her argument. Such
methods were appropriate for a professor of sociology of religion,
which she was at Candler School of Theology at Emory University
until her death at only forty-four. Eiesland's work is rooted in disability
identity and disability pride and in many ways exemplifies the spirit
of this moment in disability activism because of her celebration of
diverse embodiments and differing mobilities, as well as her focus
on physical disability. Eiesland's book is one of the first published

---

[1]Nancy Eiesland, *The Disabled God: Toward a Liberatory Theology of Disability*
(Nashville, TN: Abingdon Press, 1994).

in disability studies in the United States. What are often considered foundational texts in disability criticism were published after her book: Lennard Davis's *Enforcing Normalcy* in 1995 and Garland-Thomson's *Extraordinary Bodies* in 1996.[2]

Definition of Terms and Disability Studies

Eiesland's book, like many published works in disability theology, dedicates substantial space to definitions, models for approaching disability, surveying the field of disability studies, and featuring specific examples of the lived experiences of people with disabilities.[3] These works also provide some history of the disability rights movement and legislation, and highlight ways in which the church has lagged behind these advances, for example by obtaining exemptions from particular non-discrimination acts and architectural access requirements.[4]

I will not retrace all that ground here, but for readers new to the field of disability studies I will offer a few brief summaries. First it is common to distinguish between the terms "disability" and "impairment." "Impairment" typically refers to the physical or cognitive condition itself, while "disability" often refers primarily to the impact of social structures upon impaired bodies. These social conditions are "disabling" to bodies and minds that navigate the world in less typical ways. Examples of the disabling effects of socio-cultural structures include how lack of ramps and elevators would

---

[2]Lennard J. Davis, *Enforcing Normalcy: Disability, Deafness, and the Body* (London: Verso, 1995). Rosemarie Garland-Thomson, *Extraordinary Bodies: Figuring Disability in American Cultural and Literature* (New York: Columbia University Press, 1996).
[3]Other examples of this approach include Amos Yong's impressive *Theology and Down Syndrome: Reimagining Disability in Late Modernity* (Waco, TX: Baylor University Press, 2007), in which Yong does not begin to address doctrinal construction until page 155, and dedicates less than half of his text to theology itself (approximately 137 pages). See also Jennie Weiss Block, *Copious Hosting* (New York: Continuum, 2002), which is divided almost evenly between the disability movement and her proposal for a theology of access. Hans S. Reinders's book *Receiving the Gift of Friendship: Profound Disability, Theological Anthropology, and Ethics* (Grand Rapids. MI: Eerdmans, 2008) is structured similarly: Part 1: "Profound Disability"; Part 2: "Theology"; Part 3: "Ethics."
[4]Eiesland, *The Disabled God*, 67.

disable a person in a wheelchair, how lack of audio description or image descriptions are disabling for people with low or no vision, or how rigid academic structures and timelines are disabling for some who are neurodivergent. Stigma is constructed and socialized: consider for example how society deems hearing aids less tolerable than glasses. The way society is structured, and the way cultures respond to particular body-minds creates disabling conditions.

This distinction of terms is common to an approach to disability known as the "social model," which views persons with disabilities as an oppressed and marginalized social group and sees social structures and bias as the locus for correction and change instead of the impairment itself. This model demonstrates how disability is constructed through social and cultural values, structures, and policies.

The social model stands in contrast to the "medical model," which looks at the impairment as something to be cured, fixed, or overcome (a model of which disability studies is highly critical). The medical model serves to "enforce normalcy," endeavoring to manipulate a body-mind with impairments to conform as closely as possible to the expectations of the "norm." This approach comes with a dehumanizing, pathologizing gaze and locates the problem within the embodiment of the individual while ignoring social and structural oppressions. Such an approach often reinforces these oppressions through the elevation of the able-bodied "norm."

More recently leading thinkers are developing approaches that avoid pitting these models against each other. British scholar Tom Shakespeare, for example, raises concern that the social model may at times not account for the reality that an impairment may carry pain and real difficulty not produced strictly by social barriers or the medicalized approach. He writes, "A social constructionist approach that loses contact with the physical does us no favours. I think we have to have a position that recognizes difference, and limitation, and the very real problems which disabled people may have with their bodies and their lack of function."[5] An approach like Shakespeare's also accommodates the differences among the bodies, lives, and experiences of people with disabilities. An overly simplistic social model that focuses exclusively on physical and attitudinal barriers by a nondisabled majority culture, leaves little

---

[5]Tom Shakespeare, "Disabled Sexuality: Toward Rights and Recognition," *Sexuality and Disability* 18 (3) (2000): 159–66 (p. 62).

space for the great range of impairment and experience. People will have different experiences of their impairments based on race, class, gender, sexuality, and a range of other factors including whether the impairment is acquired or congenital. If acquired, the way it was acquired and the age of onset will result in differing experiences of the impairment as well. And of course there are the vast differences of impairments themselves and different communities associated with some impairments. Those with mobility, intellectual, or sensory impairments will encounter different social barriers. Shakespeare still affirms that "the social response and cultural meaning" of an impairment "will usually be the critical element," but he wants to save space for "the differences between different groups and individuals in the disabled community."[6] Similarly Alison Kafer is "critical of the medical model," but says she is "equally wary of a complete rejection of medical interventions."[7] She raises concern about the ways in which the discourse can negate the experiences of those whose chronic pain and fatigue is not socially constructed and is not a result of social barriers. Changes in attitudes and architecture will not relieve pain, fatigue, or illness. She says that an inflexible social model can create an environment where those who seek medical interventions or cures feel themselves a shame to the disability movement, as some assume this is a surrender to the medical industrial complex and the medical framing of our embodiments.

Themes in Disability Theology

Scholars in biblical studies were early to adopt critical textual readings with insights from disability studies, as the biblical literature has often positioned impairment as something to be fixed, so that Jesus' power could be manifest, or God could be glorified in the healing. In addition to interpretations of biblical texts, much of the focus of the theological literature is on full ecclesial inclusion and thus on both architectural and attitudinal barriers. The concern is not only with access to all church spaces—the choir

---

[6]Shakespeare, "Disabled Sexuality," 62.
[7]Alison Kafer, *Feminist, Queer, Crip* (Bloomington: University of Indiana Press, 2013), 4.

loft, the chancel, altar rail, or other elevated features in the church building—but with full participation in the life and leadership of the church. This change would require not only physical structural alterations, but a shift in language and attitudes toward people with disabilities. Thus, these works often confront impairment metaphors rife in liturgical practice: reference to sin as disease, to the human condition as crippled or broken, and to salvation as healing. For example, common expressions such as "I was blind but now I see!" figures blindness as a state of sin or alienation from God and sight as salvation.

Disability theology confronts the church's narratives, likely influenced by a cultural and literary tradition that figures people with disabilities not as typical persons with ordinary lives and desires but either as exemplars of virtue and innocence or as pitiable creatures in need of charity. Eiesland devotes a significant portion of her book calling out "disabling theologies": those theologies that prevent full inclusion, stigmatize people with impaired bodies, and construe the lives of people with disabilities as pitiable, virtuous, or sinful. Similarly Sharon Betcher charges that theology hides its "resentment of suffering as a condition of becoming," through its construal of "disability as 'brokenness,'" and "its own fixation on healing the 'in/valid'."[8] Thus disability approaches actively resist this "redemptive fix/ation," found both in medicine and in theology, as well as the narratives and "metaphysics of perfection" found in the story of Eden and the eschatological "Ever After."[9]

The creation story told in Augustinian perspective is often of a perfection where theologians assume no impairment would exist, and a fall into sin that brought with it the potential for impairment; eternal salvation then becomes a return to a perfection better even than before, and thus without the possibility of impairment through another Fall. Thus, all body-minds will be as originally intended, according to that narrative anyway, perfect in beauty, symmetry, and intelligence. Therefore disabilities often appear in theology in the context of punishment for sin, a result of the Fall and the sin of Eve and Adam, which is thought to usher in sickness, pain, and impairments, marring the perfection of original creation. However,

---

[8]Sharon Betcher, "Crip/tography: Disability Theology in the Ruins of God," *JCRT* 15 (2) (Spring 2016): 101.
[9]Betcher, "Crip/tography," 102.

disability theologians resist the assumption that their work must account for theodicy. Disability theology is not a justification of the goodness and/or power of God in the face of physical, mental, or intellectual impairment. If this were necessary, how could theology ever move beyond the perpetual relegation of impairment to devastating tragedy, suffering, and a site of pity or charity. Such an approach would be a "disabling theology," rather than a theology that challenges the negative valuation of embodiments that are outside the ideals of perfection and normalcy. This is not to say that theologians should not address theodicy in relationship to profound disability and chronic pain. Creamer's work points to this tension as she herself avoids questions of theodicy in her book *Disability and Christian Theology*.[10] Yet Creamer is critical of Sallie McFague's theology that identifies disability as simply a normal part of the created order, which elides the role of social structures and attitudes in creating disabling conditions, attitudes, and stigmas. Limits are a natural and normal part of the created order, bodies experience a range of different limits and abilities, so at which point do particular limits warrant theodicy? Where is the line that makes a particular embodiment necessitate a justification of God's goodness? This book will not attempt to find that line.

Theology written intentionally with disability in perspective is rapidly expanding and deepening. The field has produced many important works in biblical studies and studies of the ancient world.[11] Numerous volumes have come from practical and pastoral theology, primarily guiding readers in how to minister to people with disabilities and their caregivers,[12] though growing work by

---

[10]Debra Creamer, *Disability and Christian Thought: Embodied Limits and Constructive Possibilities* (Oxford: Oxford University Press, 2009).

[11]See for example Hector Avalos, *Illness and Health Care in the Ancient Near East: The Role of the Temple in Greece, Mesopotamia, and Israel* (Atlanta, GA: Scholars Press, 1995). Jeremy Schipper, *Disability Studies and the Hebrew Bible: Figuring Mephibosheth in David's Story* (New York: T&T Clark, 2006), and *Disability and Isaiah's Suffering Servant* (Oxford: Oxford University Press, 2011). *This Abled Body: Rethinking Disabilities in Biblical Studies*, ed. Hector Avalos, Sarah J. Melcher, and Jeremy Schipper (Atlanta, GA: Society of Biblical Literature, 2007). Rebecca Raphael, *Biblical Corpora: Representations of Disability in Hebrew Biblical Literature* (New York: T&T Clark, 2008). Candida R. Moss and Jeremy Schipper, eds., *Disability Studies and Biblical Literature* (New York: Palgrave Macmillan, 2011).

[12]See the many publications by John Swinton in practical theology and disability, including *Dementia: Living in the Memory of God* (Grand Rapids, MI: Eerdmans, 2012), and *Becoming Friends of Time: Disability, Timefullness, and Gentle*

theologians with disabilities are addressing the need of supporting leaders with disabilities.[13] Additionally, publications in theological ethics, including medical and bioethics, address disability using a range of methodologies.[14] The breadth of theological disciplines cover physical, mental, sensory, developmental, and intellectual disabilities. As yet, however, few works have been published in constructive theology with the concerns of disability in view.[15]

Discipleship (Waco, TX: Baylor University Press, 2016). Lamar Hardwick, *Disability and the Church: A Vision for Diversity and Inclusion* (Downers Grove, IL: IVP, 2021). Sarah Jean Barton, *Becoming the Baptized Body: Disability and the Practice of Christian Community* (Waco, TX: Baylor University Press, 2022). Erin Raffety, *From Inclusion to Justice: Disability, Ministry, and Congregational Leadership* (Waco, TX: Baylor University Press, 2022). Jennie Weiss Block, *Copious Hosting: A Theology of Access for Persons with Disabilities* (New York: Continuum, 2002). Rebecca Spurrier, *The Disabled Church: Human Difference and the Art of Communal Worship* (New York: Fordham. University Press, 2019).

[13]See for example the work of Miriam Spies. Miriam Spies, "Making Space, Offering Voice: Leadership of People with Disabilities in God's Mission," *International Review of Missions* 108 (1) (June 2019): 25–37; and Miriam Spies, "Liturgical Imagination at Full Stretch: Possibilities for Leadership of Disabled People," *Concilium* 5 (2020): 128–37.

[14]Hans S. Reinders *Receiving the Gift of Friendship: Profound Disability, Theological Anthropology, and Ethics* (Grand Rapids, MI: Eerdmans, 2008), and *Disability, Providence, and Ethics: Bridging Gaps, Transforming Lives* (Waco, TX: Baylor University Press, 2014). Devan Stahl, *Disability's Challenge to Theology: Genes, Eugenics, and the Metaphysics of Modern Medicine* (South Bend, IN: University of Notre Dame Press, 2022). See also various publications by Stanley Hauerwas on intellectual disability, including *Suffering Presence: Theological Reflections on Medicine, the Mentally Handicapped, and the Church* (South Bend, IN: University of Notre Dame Press, 1986) and the volume edited by John Swinton, *Critical Reflections on Stanley Hauerwas' Theology of Disability: Disabling Society, Enabling Theology* (Binghampton, NY: Haworth Pastoral Press, 2004).

[15]One early notable exception is Yong, *Theology and Down Syndrome*. Other recent additions addressing doctrine in some form include Brian Brock, *Wondrously Wounded: Theology, Disability, and the Body of Christ* (Waco, TX: Baylor University Press, 2020); David McLachlan, *Accessible Atonement: Disability, Theology, and the Cross of Christ* (Waco, TX: Baylor University Press, 2021). As Creamer noted in 2003: "An informed perspective that critically reflects on disability as a primary source for constructive theology is needed, including, for example, the nature of humanity and of God." ("Toward a Theology That Includes the Human Experience of Disability," *Journal of Religion, Disability, and Health* v. 7.3 (2003): 57–67 (pp. 63–4). And again in 2009 Creamer notes that "discussions about disability and religion are still in their infancy" and that "theologians have been largely absent from discussions of images of God that are relevant to the experience of disability." Debra Creamer, *Disability and Christian Theology: Embodied Limits and Constructive Possibilities* (Oxford: Oxford University Press, 2009), 88.

The Disabled God

The Disabled God, written originally as a master's thesis, is limited in terms of doctrinal development, yet was tremendously influential in the nascent field of disability theology. Eiesland's passionate affirmation of impaired bodies as *imago dei* and the demand for access, especially architectural and liturgical, inspired many readers, and her ideas forged a path for the inclusion of disability perspectives in theological studies. Her work is so influential that Deborah Creamer noted in 2009 that "almost every text or article on religion and disability published after Eiesland's book ... includes a reference to the Disabled God,"[16] and that trend has continued. Tim Basselin, for example, wrote in 2011 that "Christ, and thus God, as disabled is the starting point for any theology of disability."[17] And a session of the Religion and Disability Studies Unit at the Annual Meeting of the American Academy of Religion in 2020 was devoted to considering the impact of Eiesland's book twenty-five years after its publication.

Eiesland's work has engendered both approval and critique: some find it a liberating concept, and others consider it heretical speculation or subjective projection. Regardless, the book was a groundbreaking text, putting the perspective and experience of people with disabilities at the forefront of Christian interpretation. Creamer remarks: "The memorable image of the Disabled God, as one who intimately knows and even experiences disability, is especially important: in addition to calling for change, it irrevocably changes the way one encounters the Christian story. How can one be a Christian and not value experiences of disability? The image necessarily leads to changes in understanding and in action."[18]

Eiesland says her book was inspired by a kind of vision she had of God in a puff-chair, the sort of wheelchair that is controlled by the breath of the user. For Eiesland, this vision does not disclose a pitiable God or suffering servant, but an active God, one on the move. She rejects traditional notions of God's omnipotence, but her

---

[16]Creamer, *Disability and Christian Theology*, 87.

[17]Timothy Basselin, "Why Theology Needs Disability," *Theology Today* 68 (1) (2011): 47–57 (p. 53).

[18]Debra Creamer, "Theological Accessibility: The Contribution of Disability," *Disability Studies Quarterly* 26 (4) (Fall 2006), https://dsq-sds.org/article/view/812/987 (accessed October 18, 2022).

theology does not leave God without power and ability. She offers an icon that resists the projection of idealized human power and unrestrained force. She explains that when she saw God this way, "I beheld God as survivor, unpitying and forthright. I recognized the incarnate Christ in the image of those judged 'not feasible,' 'unemployable,' with 'questionable quality of life.' Here was God for me."[19] She goes on to qualify her use of "survivor" here to describe God, because the word is culturally "contaminated with notions of victimization, radical individualism, and alienation, as well as with an ethos of virtuous suffering."[20] When she associates God disclosed in Jesus with a "survivor," she explains this is an image of "a simple, unself-pitying, honest body, for whom the limits of power are palpable but not tragic."[21]

I hurry to add that I am not going to argue here that it would be apt for people to consider God disabled because it is a beneficial image for people with disabilities—and neither is that Eiesland's argument, despite what some of her critics charge, although she does find comfort in God so imagined. I will argue that this understanding of God derives from the revelation of God in Jesus. Truly Eiesland's proposal is not fully developed. The general suggestion that God is disabled because Jesus Christ is resurrected in an impaired body does not in and of itself stand up to the expectations of most theological method. But she does more than what some of her critics claim. Her project is not simply the result of her subjective projections. Her focus is primarily on access and full inclusion into the leadership of the church and less on doctrinal revision and development, but her suggestions are fruitful for theological reconstruction nonetheless.

Eiesland's claim that God is disabled rests upon the significance of the physical impairment visible in the resurrected Christ's hands and feet and obscured or hidden on his side.[22] According to Eiesland his resurrected body is not a "perfected" body, as in an idealized, perfectly "able" body without brokenness or impairment. The resurrected body with which he returns to the Father, for Eiesland,

---

[19]Eiesland, *The Disabled God*, 89.
[20]Eiesland, *The Disabled God*, 102.
[21]Eiesland, *The Disabled God*, 102.
[22]She makes the connection here to visible disability and those disabling conditions that are often hidden, like chronic pain that may not be visible in the physical comport of the one enduring it.

is a disabled body. She makes four constructive theological claims that will be foundational for the theology developed throughout this book.

First, Jesus reveals true humanity, and thus as one with physical impairment, he both discloses "the reality that full personhood is fully compatible with the experience of disability," and demonstrates that persons with disabilities are created *imago dei*.[23] Here in her theological anthropology, she shares with nearly all disability theology an intentional emphasis on embodiment.

Second, Jesus as God incarnate, who retains the wounds of his crucifixion into the resurrected life, means that God is disabled, which simultaneously reinforces the claim that people with disabilities are created in the image of God. Here in her bold assertion of God's disabled body, Eiesland does not carefully specify how this relates to the Trinity or to God's second "person." This is something I endeavor to correct in the chapters that follow.

Third, our central symbol and sacrament, the bodily practice of Eucharist, relies upon the impairment of the flesh of Jesus. In the Eucharist, the body of Christ remains broken, and is perpetually broken anew at the table with his words "this is my body broken for you." Jesus, the disabled God, remains bodily present in the church particularly in this sacrament of his impaired flesh.[24] Eiesland calls out the hypocrisy of a church gathering at this table while refusing to dismantle barriers to disabled inclusion, writing: "The dissonance raised by the nonacceptance of persons with disabilities and the acceptance of grace through Christ's broken body necessitates that the church find new ways of interpreting disability."[25] So too Eiesland identifies the church itself as a body impaired, or as Eiesland calls it, a "community of struggle."

Last, Jesus is the "first fruits" of the resurrected life, the first to receive the resurrected body, and because he retains his impairments, one can expect the resurrected life to include disabled bodies. This means that "resurrection is not about the negation or erasure of our disabled bodies in hopes of perfect images, untouched by physical disability; rather Christ's resurrection offers hope that our

---

[23]Eiesland, *Disabled God*, 99–100.
[24]Eiesland, *Disabled God*, 23.
[25]Eiesland, *Disabled God*, 23.

nonconventional, and sometimes difficult, bodies participate fully in the *imago Dei* and that God is ... touched by our experience."[26]

Critiques of Eielsand

Similar to the growth of disciplines like African American Studies and Women's Studies following the Civil Rights and Women's Movements, Disability Studies likewise developed with the activism and identity-pride of the movement. And similar to the ways in which White feminism and Black Power movements of that era endured critique from Black women and women of color, so too some of the early emphases of the disability movement are challenged by subsequent scholarship. Eiesland's book is in many ways a product of its time early in the development of disability studies, before the development of Crip theory and the intentional inclusion of intersectional analysis. Not all working in the field of disability theology are receptive to Eiesland's contributions. In what follows I will address some criticisms of Eiesland's work, focusing especially on the influential critique of John Swinton, who is a leading voice in the field, and place Eiesland's book within the context of its time and within the field of disability studies.[27]

A number of scholars have denounced Eiesland's explicit focus on physical impairments to the exclusion of other disabilities in her book. Others question whether her proposal that God bears disability within the divine life would apply to significant intellectual disability.[28] It is one thing to note that Jesus eternally retains piercings in his hands, feet, and side, or to portray God's mobility as similar to those using assistive technology, and quite another to consider God without supreme intelligence. And as disability studies grows in its inclusion of mental illness and mad studies, some ask how these experiences figure into this image of God as disabled, which Eiesland doesn't begin to address. Does her work perpetuate a harmful division between differing forms of disability? Does it reinforce a hierarchy of impairment, with intellectual disability relegated to the bottom and most feared position?

---

[26]Eiesland, *Disabled God*, 107.

[27]John Swinton, "Who Is the God We Worship? Theologies of Disability: Challenges and New Possibilities," *International Journal of Practical Theology* 14 (2) (2011): 273–307.

[28]Debra Creamer, Amos Yong, John Swinton, and Hans Reinders raise this concern.

Eiesland is not silent on this issue; she calls for the church to "hold our bodies together," and explains that such a stance means "not distinguishing between 'good' and 'bad' disabilities," and "refusing to stigmatize people with intellectual disabilities as inherently more impaired than those with ambulatory disabilities."[29] Admittedly, however, she does limit her theological work primarily to physical disability. While this critique is valid, I believe when her work is situated in the context in which it arose, this shortcoming is not justified but better understood. Similar charges are raised against much early disability activism, which focused especially on physical disability and access to support "independent living." Disability movements that emphasize independence and autonomy as ultimate goals, just as with feminist movements with similar aims, unwittingly participate in structures that oppress others, and Eiesland's work is probably situated there, written in the 1990s. However, disability justice work in recent decades has advanced beyond this, and calls for radical change, not just a more expansive understanding of what is acceptable or normative. Disability studies as an academic discipline shows a similar reflex toward physical impairment. For example, a 2014 article in the *Disability Studies Quarterly* found that within its publication physical disability was typically presumed with the word "disability," and thus was not given a qualifier, while mental disability or intellectual disability was given the specificity in keywords and article titles.[30]

In an effort to assert a positive valuation of disabled bodies, the disability rights movement early on focused on countering the narratives of pity and devaluation with celebrations of impaired embodiment, which some consider a romanticized portrayal of disability that may belie experiences of chronic pain and prolonged sickness. Not all people with disabilities celebrate their impairment in the way that some authors and disability activists encourage, which may leave some people with disability feeling they are a disappointment to the movement, unable to live up to the expectation of the ableist social norm, nor the ideals of positive body images within the disability rights movement. Alison Kafer explains, "A crip refusal to see disability as tragedy, as traumatic, can be just as restricting on

---

[29]Eiesland, *Disabled God*, 96.
[30]Elizabeth Brewer and Brenda Jo Brueggemann, "The View from DSQ," *Disability Studies Quarterly* 23 (2) (2014), https://dsq-sds.org/article/view/4258/3598 (accessed October 18, 2022).

our politics and our theories as the ableist insistence that disability is always and only tragic."[31] Similarly Mia Mingus writes:

> I don't in general like body positivity. When I think about my disability, it's not something I need to feel positive or negative about. If we didn't live in an ableist society, we would recognize that our bodies are all different and have different capacities. Most of us are trying to squeeze our bodies into capitalism. I don't want to be wearing my "I heart disability" sandwich board and ringing my bell all the time. There are hard things about disability and that's okay. Bodies are amazing and gross and weird and strange—why do we have to be so positive about it? Why is it so important for us to feel that way?[32]

Nirmala Erevelles describes this as a process through which people with impairments are expected to undergo, a kind of conscientization that results in their claiming of disability identity and a pride in their bodies. This universalizing expectation of people with disabilities that comes typically from North American disability scholars and activists to people in the South also doesn't easily translate in some communities of color in the United States.[33] Not all people live in situations that give them the freedom or privilege to proudly claim a Crip identity, something Mingus and Erevelles both note particularly among disabled people of color.[34] Mingus writes: "Over and over I meet disabled women of color who do not identify as disabled, even though they have the lived reality of being disabled. And this is for many complicated reasons around race, ability, gender, access, etc. It can be very dangerous to identify as disabled when your survival depends on you denying it."[35]

---

[31]Kafer, *Feminist, Queer, Crip*, 6.

[32]Mia Mingus in an interview by ALOK for *Them* magazine, https://www.them.us/story/ugliness-disability-mia-mingus.

[33]Nirmala Erevelles, "The Color of Violence: Reflecting on Gender, Race, and Disability in Wartime," in *Feminist Disability Studies*, ed. Kim Q. Hall (Bloomington: Indiana University Press, 2011): 118–35.

[34]Nirmala Erevelles, *Disability and Difference in Global Contexts: Enabling a Transformative Body Politic* (New York: Palgrave Macmillan, 2011).

[35]Mia Mingus, "Moving toward the Ugly: A Politics Beyond Desirability," https://leavingevidence.wordpress.com/2011/.

Eiesland's book may be guilty of such romanticization, as her proposal is challenged by those who do not rejoice in their embodiment, who do seek healing, and those for whom the idea of an eternity in their impaired body is anything but hopeful. Though Eielsand is not entirely silent on the struggle some may have with their impairment, perhaps particularly when it is obtained later in life, by featuring the experience of Nancy Mairs, a woman with MS. Though Eiesland includes Mairs's accounts of depression and suicidal ideation, she doesn't do much to reckon with the vast difference of impairment and experience in her account, including the reality that impairments are often created through traumatic events, including Jesus' own horrific wounding.

Related to the romantization of impairment is the tendency to naturalize impairment as a path to social acceptance of diverse embodiments. This is something I've done, for example, with my daughter when she sees someone with non-typical mobility, and she shows extreme curiosity about their body; I explain that humans have many different types of bodies, much like she was born with a heart that is different from her brother's. However, emphasizing impairment as part of nature, typically congenital or acquired through illness or aging, erases the sociopolitical conditions that sanction and enact violence and economic policies that perpetuate extreme poverty, which are root causes of much disability worldwide.[36] Thus naturalization, while serving a purpose for disability pride, potentially erases traumatic histories at the root of the impairment or related to the trauma from the medical treatment of it.[37] What percentage of disability in our world is due to war and state-sponsored violence?[38] How have colonial and geopolitical processes produced so-called "natural impairments?" For instance, according to a 2004 study, "indigenous populations

---

[36]See Karen Soldatic and Shaun Grech, "Transnationalising Disability Studies: Rights, Justice, and Impairments," *Disability Studies Quarterly* 34 (2) (2014), https://dsq-sds.org/article/view/4249/3588 (accessed October 18, 2022).

[37]See Alison Kafer, "Un/Safe Disclosures: Scenes of Disability and Trauma," *Journal of Literary and Cultural Disability Studies* 10 (1) (2016): 1–20. Critics of the social model note that this approach often ignores the "presence and persistence of pain" as well as how the impairment occurred, possibly in a traumatic event. In this model a "traumatically induced impairment" is treated no differently than a congenital impairment.

[38]See Jasbir K. Puar, *The Right to Maim: Debility, Capacity, and Disability* (Durham, NC: Duke University Press, 2017).

within white settler societies have the highest levels of congenital impairment."[39] Consider also the levels of chronic illness and cancer that are related to environmental racism and the toxic pollution dumped in communities with concentrated Brown and Black populations. In what sense are these impairments "natural"?

Eiesland is not entirely silent on these issues either, as she notes at least once that Jesus' impairment is the result of torture by talking of Jesus' "disfigured side" and the "internal damage wrought by hacking swords" as a perspective that necessitates a "deromanticizing" of Jesus' impaired body.[40] She also notes in her discussion of the Eucharist that the one we remember in the sacrament is one who was "physically tortured."[41] And in this bodily practice of bread and wine we recognize the one who identifies with those who "have struggled to maintain the integrity and dignity of their bodies in the face of the physical mutilation of injustice and rituals of bodily degradation."[42] She makes a few passing references to political and economic causes of disability, and calls for disability activism to include protesting war and global economic policies that create poverty and malnourishment: "Only institutionalized violence and systematic torture can explain why malnutrition is the primary cause of disability worldwide. ... Bearing witness for peace and struggling against the weapons trade, a liberatory theology of disability calls for an end to the violence which tears at bodies

---

[39]Soldatic and Grech summarize:

> According to researchers such as O'Leary (2004) indigenous populations within white settler societies have the highest levels of congenital impairment. In Australia, over half of the indigenous population has an impairment or long-term health condition (Australian Bureau of Statistics, 2010). While impairment was a common feature of indigenous societies prior to the arrival of the white colonial settler ..., the disproportionate prevalence of impairment caused by (neo)colonial violence has been met with silence in the global instruments of disability justice. In a similar fashion, the vast impairment caused by a US-instigated 36-year civil war in Guatemala, especially among the indigenous population, remains unquestioned and untargeted, excluded from national disability instruments and policies.

C. M. O'Leary, "Fetal Alcohol Syndrome: Diagnosis, Epidemiology, and Developmental Outcomes," *Journal of Paediatrics and Child Health* 40 (1 and 2) (2004): 2–7. ABS. *See* Australian Bureau of Statistics.
[40]Eiesland, *Disabled God*, 101.
[41]Eiesland, *Disabled God*, 101.
[42]Eiesland, *Disabled God*, 102.

and multiplies refugees."[43] Nonetheless it is true that throughout her work the wounds in Jesus' flesh after the resurrection become symbols of the acceptance of disability in the life of God and a breaking of the stigma and taboo around impaired bodies, such that she could be guilty of romanticizing the torture that produced these icons. For example, she writes that his gesture toward the disciples to touch his broken body "alters the taboo of physical avoidance of disability," but overall her account does not reckon with the violence and trauma that produced this broken body.[44]

While Eiesland's argument largely hinges on the wounds in Jesus' resurrected body, some question whether these marks actually constitute a disability. John Swinton, for example, finds the resurrected body of Jesus to be particularly problematic for Eiesland's claims because his resurrected body is not functionally impaired but is actually capable of more than it was before the wounding: now he can pass through walls, suddenly appear, and disappear. Swinton additionally argues that the resurrection itself is "quite a display of ability!"[45] Here he attributes the resurrection to Jesus' own act or ability.

Swinton may be correct that pointing to Jesus' resurrected wounds, which some refer to as scars, makes a weak case for a disabled Jesus. However, he ignores the role the Eucharist plays in Eiesland's argument. Jesus declares that his body is broken until he returns, and the tradition declares it perpetually broken in the ongoing memory and life of the church at least until the final resurrection. Perhaps Jesus' resurrected body itself is not an image of this-worldly disability as it is transformed as the "first fruits" of the promised Kingdom. However, the corporate body of Christ and the Eucharist as images of Jesus' broken body surely indicate an ongoing impairment. Further, I find his claim that Jesus' resurrection is a sign of Jesus' ability to be misleading, as the biblical witness and tradition point to either the Father or the Spirit as the one to resurrect Jesus, so one could just as easily claim that Jesus' resurrection is a sign of his dependence, of his lack of power, and of his need, as he relied on the Holy Spirit or the Father to raise him.

---

[43]Eiesland, *Disabled God*, 97.
[44]Eiesland, *Disabled God*, 101.
[45]Swinton, "Who Is the God We Worship," 284.

Swinton affirms that it may make sense to speak of a disability in terms of the incarnation and crucifixion but not of the resurrection; yet he also argues that such a reading of Jesus' wounds doesn't comport with traditional interpretations of the crucifixion. He writes, "Importantly, within mainstream theology, the scars of Jesus are perceived as a source of hope and salvation as they remind Christians of the meaning of Jesus' sacrifice and the reality of their redemption. Jesus' scars are marks of redemption and hope, not of oppression or disability."[46] To suggest that Jesus' scars are for Eiesland a sign of his oppression, is to misread her, as her central point is quite explicitly that impaired bodies are not in themselves the locus of suffering—it is the social response to those bodies that creates the oppression. Jesus' wounds, holding them out to his friends to touch, demonstrates the overturning of such stigmas in the resurrected life, thus signaling that impaired bodies are not sites of oppression or suffering in a context that does not devalue particular identities based on a culturally constructed norm. In the resurrected life, impairment isn't a sign of suffering and oppression. God embracing that identity in Christ demonstrates a different value system, and an identity grounded not on a measure of ability or normativity, but measured by one's proximity to Jesus, or as we will discuss in the last chapter, one's incorporation into this particular body of Jesus.

Further Swinton's argument that according to "mainstream theology" Jesus' scars are not marks of his oppression disregards the insights of many Christians and theologians who see in Jesus' crucifixion, not a sign of his willing sacrifice for our redemption, but the result of sinful structures that enact violence on those who upset the status quo, powers, and norms of the day. For example, James Cone's account of *The Cross and Lynching Tree* demonstrates the various ways in which tormented and oppressed bodies connect with Jesus' tortured and crucified body, looking to the cross not as a simple mark of hope or locus of salvation, but as a deep solidarity with the persecuted.[47] The resurrection is the word of hope and the promise that oppression doesn't get the last word, but the crucifixion is a site of suffering. Those wounds on Jesus' resurrected body

---

[46]Swinton, "Who Is the God We Worship," 285.
[47]James H. Cone, *The Cross and the Lynching Tree* (Maryknoll, NY: Orbis Books, 2011).

are important, not only to show that it was truly Jesus who was resurrected, but also as an affirmation of the inherent worth of those tortured bodies. Eiesland does not identify the resurrected scars on Jesus' body only as a mark of oppression, as Swinton suggests, but as a sign of God's identification with those whose bodies are stigmatized, surveilled, and persecuted, as well as God's victory over those forces of oppression.

One of Swinton's critiques that I find more compelling is that Jesus' suffering and rejection was not on account of his impairments, but at most his body became impaired because he was persecuted, not vice versa. Jesus did not endure the social stigma of living in a disabled body. This seems right, and yet Jesus was persecuted both because of his particular embodied identity and his outspoken rejection of certain social, cultural, and religious norms of his day, so his experience may share some communal similarities. Many have noted that Jesus is not the epitome of masculinity and that he subverted the patriarchy of his day.[48] He doesn't fight but tells those with him to put away their swords; he doesn't marry or father children. Nor is he the icon of a non-disabled humanity, or the image of the idealized "normal" body, or "normal" human (as determined by standards of culture and society). Jesus stumbles on his way to Golgotha; he is unable to carry his cross, someone else has to do it for him. He isn't described as tall, or handsome, or strong. Nor does he have power, wealth, and prestige. He doesn't even have a home. He is dependent upon the generosity and care of others. What power he exhibits in those moments of healing, feeding, and miraculous knowledge during his ministry is not his own but the Spirit working through him for a particular purpose in each occasion.[49]

In fact, if we identify Jesus in some sense with the suffering servant of Isaiah 53, we have even more reason to consider him among those outcast and possibly a part of the disability community

---

[48]See Sharon V. Betcher, *Spirit and the Politics of Disablement* (Minneapolis, MN: Fortress Press, 2007), 75, and Sharon Betcher, "Crip/tography: Disability Theology in the Ruins of God," *JCRT* 15 (2) (Spring 2016): 101. See also Rosemary Radford Ruether, *Sexism and Godtalk* (Boston: Beacon Press, 1983) and Sandra M. Schneiders, *Women and the Word: The Gender of God in New Testament and Spirituality of Women* (New York: Paulist Press, 1986).
[49]Theological support for this reading of Jesus' miracles will be developed in later chapters.

broadly conceived. While it is not exegetically accurate to identify the suffering servant directly with the person of Jesus, it is certainly true that Christians have read this figure as a representation of the person of Jesus for centuries, especially in prayer and liturgy. The suffering servant is described as someone with significant disfigurement. Jeremy Schipper translates the passage: "marred was his appearance, unlike human semblance, and his form unlike that of mortals."[50] This person was "despised and withdrew from humanity; a man of sufferings and acquainted with diseases; and like someone who hides their faces from us, he was despised and we held him of no account."[51] Schipper argues persuasively that this disfigurement was not the result of abuse but is given by God, and according to Schipper this individual is not simply a nondisabled person who becomes disabled but is someone who experiences the social impact of disability. This person, in his disfigurement, experiences disabling stigma, rejection, and social isolation. Here is God in Christ. So while it is true that Jesus' social suffering was not due to a significant impairment, one may still be able to locate his experience within the larger community of the disabled.

This question of Jesus' status as one of the disability community is anachronistic, of course, as the coalition building of disability activism is a modern movement, but it may help to understand the debate and parameters around claiming status as disabled happening today. What counts as disability and who can claim membership with the disability community is debated, with some advocating open or loose borders that recognize the fluidity within disability, while others voice concern about the political consequences of an overly porous boundary where we could all claim disabled status at some point or another without ever facing the social and economic consequences of disability. Carrie Sandhal, along with Robert McRuer, suggests it may be possible for nondisabled allies to identify with "Crip." The term "Crip" has already expanded in application beyond those who would be deemed "crippled" with a mobility impairment to include sensory, mental, and intellectual impairments, such that Sandahl sees "Crip" like "Queer" to be "fluid and ever-changing, claimed by those whom it did not originally

---

[50]Jeremy Schipper's translation, *Disability and Isaiah's Suffering Servant* (Oxford: Oxford University Press, 2011), 3.
[51]Schipper, *Disability and Isaiah's Suffering Servant*, 3.

define."[52] Alison Kafer also pushes on this boundary, considering the ways in which disability communities also include family members, such as Hearing Children of Deaf Adults, or CODAs, who consider themselves part of Deaf communities, with some even claiming Deaf identity, while not themselves being deaf or hard-of-hearing.[53] She argues for a relational model that recognizes that families of persons with disabilities are also included in this community, along with lovers or friends, as they often share the stigma and isolation experienced by individuals with disability.

Kafer also moves the discussion away from strictly definable guidelines for what "counts" as a disability and toward that of a "collective affinity," so that the discussion includes not only those with physical and sensory impairment but also those who experience chronic illness, intellectual disability, and mental illness. What is the rubric by which we measure disability? Is it that which is handed to us by the medical industry? Does it require a diagnosis? How do we qualify those who go in and out of symptoms, whose cancer is in remission, or who experience temporary impairments during each recurrence of the disease? What about a person with a visible difference such as a large birthmark that has "no bearing on their physical capabilities, but that often prompt discriminatory treatment?"[54] She asks if we can imagine "a 'we' that includes folks who identify as or with disabled people but don't themselves 'have' a disability."[55] The relational/political model she proposes retains some of the fluidity of Crip identity found in the work of Sandhal and McRuer, focusing on the benefit for political action if we gather more people to the work: "to claim crip critically is to recognize the ethical, epistemic, and political responsibilities behind such claims."[56] Yet she is also cautious that a stance that claims "we are *all* disabled" is a deeply ableist declaration that obscures the "structural inequality or patterns of exclusion and discrimination."[57] Opening the circle to include more people has some advantages, but

---

[52]Carrie Sandahl, "Queering Crip or Cripping the Queer?: Intersections of Queer and Crip Identities in Solo Autobiographical Performance," *A Journal of Gay and Lesbian Studies* 9 (1–2) (2003): 25–56 (p. 27).

[53]Kafer, *Feminist, Queer, Crip*, 13.

[54]Kafer, *Feminist, Queer, Crip*, 11.

[55]Kafer, *Feminist, Queer, Crip*, 12.

[56]Kafer, *Feminist, Queer, Crip*, 13.

[57]Kafer, *Feminist, Queer, Crip*, 13.

nondisabled people claiming some sort of Crip status could blunt the political edge of the movement. These scholars seek to problematize the identity category of disability because they believe the benefits of an expanded commitment to disability justice is worth this risk of appropriation, as this move offers a "vital refusal of simplistic binaries like disabled/nondisabled and sick/healthy" upon which normativity is erected.[58] As Kafer explains, "Claiming Crip, then, can be a way of acknowledging that we all have bodies and minds with shifting abilities, and wrestling with the political meanings and histories of such shifts."[59]

I do not want to suggest that we can claim Jesus is Crip based on the fluidity of "Crip" according to some influential theorists. I do think it may be fair to consider in what sense Jesus suffered because of his opposition to certain social and political norms, and one could argue that he received his impairment because of his particular embodiment, as a poor rural Jew who spoke out against the abuse of power, the hoarding of wealth, and religious commitments that ignored those in need, including quite explicitly, those who were sick, mentally ill, and physically impaired. But further, I will argue that in Christ, God experiences need and interdependence eternally, not simply at the crucifixion and beyond but as God in God's second way of being, that is, as the Son.[60]

One of Swinton's strangest critiques of Eiesland, in my opinion, is that her insights are only for those with disabled bodies and that her claim that in Christ God is disabled is exclusionary of people who are nondisabled. He writes,

> If God is disabled in a way that is anything other than metaphorical, then presumably God can't be able-bodied? The danger here is either that we end up with a form of theology that is as exclusive as the theology it is trying to replace or challenge, or we find ourselves lost in a mass of impairment

---

[58]Kafer, *Feminist, Queer, Crip*, 13.

[59]Kafer, *Feminist, Queer, Crip*, 13.

[60]Some of the harshest of Eiesland's critics reject her proposal largely on the basis of what appears to be their precommitment to denying liberation theologies as a form of credible theological construction. Reinders claims Eiesland's theology is framed by oppositional thinking, which he identifies with liberation theologies: a binary of oppressed and oppressor. For example he calls her guilty of "the antagonistic approach of liberation theology" (Reinders, *Receiving Friendship*, 183). It should be clear that I reject Reinders's simplistic and dismissive characterization of liberation theology.

specific God images which may do political work but end up deeply theologically confusing.[61]

Hans Reinders also critiques Eiesland's theology because it does not include the nondisabled. Reinders asks repeatedly a form of the question: "What about the able-bodied" or "what role does the able-bodied play?" I strongly disagree that positing God in Christ as disabled, as will be described in what follows, is necessarily exclusionary of nondisabled people, any more than it is exclusionary of women to have to deal with the maleness of the person of Jesus in Christology. As Eiesland herself claimed, "The significance of the disabled God is not primarily maleness, but rather physicality."[62] I affirm that in our culture the resurrected Christ would in some ways be experienced as impaired or disfigured, and that rather than erase that embodiment, as the dominant theological tradition has done for centuries, we should earnestly consider what it means theologically that the humanity of God, that taken to the being of God in Christ, is a body that suffered and retained the wounds or scars of that trauma eternally. Perhaps this is not strictly a "disabled" body according to the fluid use of that term. Maybe it is more fitting to consider this in terms of embodied limits such as we find in Debra Creamer's work, or an expression of vulnerability as we have in the theology of Thomas Reynolds,[63] but regardless theology needs to confront the nature of the incarnation and the real embodiment of Jesus as the Son of God and to mark the damage done when a false ableist normativity is projected onto the humanity of God in Christ. Eiesland's proposal, developed further through a trinitarian theology, demonstrates God's being as radically formed by God's experience in Jesus as vulnerable, dependent, and in need. This doesn't mean that a specific form of impairment must be identified with the being or mind of God, but that in Christ God does truly share this common human experience. The disabled God challenges human notions of "normal," "power," "strength," and "beauty," and this is so true that God embraces weakness into God's divine life, without ceasing to be God. Weakness, dependency, receptivity, and "disfigurement" are not contrary to who God is within God's

---

[61]Swinton, "Who Is the God We Worship," 285.
[62]Eiesland, *Disabled God*, 102.
[63]Thomas Reynolds, *Vulnerable Communion*.

own being, are not foreign to the life God eternally determined for Godself.

In what follows, I will explore what it means for an interdependence to be a necessary condition for God's life by engaging an unlikely interlocutor in the field of Barth studies. I hope that by exploring the debate in theological ontology I may lay additional theological foundations for Eiesland's "disabled God" and advance her contribution to our understanding of the nature and being of God. I argue for an eternal identity of the Son that may be described as disabled, drawing not only from the resurrected wounds, but from a range of theological accounts that point to a divine mode of being that is receptive, dependent, and vulnerable.

2

Covenant Ontology and the Impaired Body of the Son

Themes in Disability Theology

In what follows I highlight a few features of Eiesland's theology, features shared with most disability theologies, that I in turn endeavor to support and strengthen in the chapters that follow through engagement with tradition and doctrine. As this book pertains primarily to the doctrine of God, and how Christology relates to trinitarian theology, in what follows I will focus on contributions from Eiesland and others as they relate specifically to understandings of God. I will consider what a disability focus on embodiment means for the humanity of God assumed in the incarnation and in what sense one can say God is interdependent and vulnerable.

Understandably the most common doctrine addressed by disability theologians is theological anthropology, with an emphasis on embodiment. As Eiesland notes, "the corporeal is for people with disabilities the most real ... That is, we become keenly aware that our physical selves determine our perceptions of the social and physical world."[1] Creamer echoes this reality: "For many of us, awareness of embodiment is a fact of life—we are always aware of our bodies because of chronic pain, muscle weakness or limited abilities."[2] Christian theology offers a rich array of resources with

---

[1] Eiesland, *Disabled God*, 31.
[2] Debra Creamer, "Finding God in Our Bodies: Theology from the Perspective of People with Disabilities, Part 2," *Journal of Religion, Disability, and Health* 2 (2) (1995): 67–87 (p. 68).

which to develop theologies of embodiment: "From the incarnation (*The Word made flesh*) and Christology *(Christ was fully human)* to the Eucharist (*This is my body, this is my blood)*, the resurrection of the body, and the church (*the body of Christ who is its head),* Christianity has been a religion *of the body.*"[3] Yet despite this fertile ground for a theological assessment of embodiment, Christianity has often been drawn to the dualism that undercuts the goodness and significance of the body. Thus, disability theologians call for an intentional turning to the body in our theological investigations.

Critical of anthropologies that would divide body and soul, such that the soul is our true self and we simply have a body, fragmenting our natures, Creamer notes often in her work: "we not only *have* bodies but *are* bodies."[4] We are not a soul encased in a body, yet we are more than just body; we are both inseparably. Creamer also highlights the necessity of bodies for the very task of theology itself. All our knowledge is mediated through our bodies, as is our experience. We experience God through the body. We use the body to think about God, and to embrace the people that mediate the love of God to us. We communicate this love, knowledge, and experience through our bodies either through words written or spoken, and/or through our countenance, our joy, and our affection. Our bodies are essential for the task of living our theological commitments in action.

Eiesland's consideration of Jesus as the embodiment of the disabled God takes the physical reality of Jesus' body seriously, as we must likewise do when we consider the implications for the being of God that the Son is embodied. As mentioned in the previous chapter, Eiesland specifically notes that the theological significance of Jesus' body is not primarily about his sexed embodiment as male but the very physicality of his existence. She continues, "Jesus Christ the disabled God, is consonant with the image of Jesus Christ the stigmatized Jew, person of color, and representative of the poor and hungry—those who have struggled to maintain the integrity and dignity of their bodies in the face of the physical mutilation of injustice and rituals of bodily degradation."[5] Jesus' Jewish identity

---

[3]Creamer, "Toward a Theology That Includes the Human Experience of Disability," 63. Emphasis in original. Also see Sallie McFague, *The Body of God: An Ecological Theology* (Minneapolis, MN: Fortress Press, 1993), 14.

[4]Creamer, "Toward A Theology That Includes the Human Experience of Disability," 62. Creamer, *Disability and Christian Theology*, 57.

[5]Eiesland, *Disabled God*, 102.

was embodied; his circumcision was of his flesh. This Jewish body and identity led to the torture of his body, resulting in the impairment of his body. He cared for people in their bodies, their hunger, their sickness, and their material poverty. This physical nature of the Son's own historical existence as Jesus and the physical nature of Jesus' ministry are central to disability Christology.

The literature of disability studies challenges Western colonial assumptions of the "normal" human as a white, nondisabled, heterosexual male of means and the imposition of this "ideal" as the standard by which all of humanity is measured and valued. Thus, much of the theological literature also brings necessary critique to Christianity's participation in and promulgation of this cultural mechanism. Disability theology denies the supremacy of the solitary, independent individual identified in much philosophy and theology, along with their portrayals of humanity as primarily mind or spirit, and the concomitant binaries that denigrate embodiment, value male over female, and so on. Disability theology also rejects the corresponding image of God as the ultimate perfection of this Western ideal human, which would figure God as supremely autonomous and self-sufficient and refuse divine vulnerability, interdependence, and mutuality. Much like Mary Daly's famous dictum, "If God is male, then the male is God,"[6] if divine freedom is utter independence, those who present lives of independence are figured closer to God than those whose embodiment situates them in need of care or assistance (be it a prosthetic, a care-giver, a drug to manage mental illness, or social assistance like food stamps and housing shelters). Because disability theologians reject self-sufficiency and independence as ultimate values, these qualities are not given supreme status as attributes of God.

Like many other disability and liberation theologians, Eiesland explicitly rejects notions of omnipotence, positing instead a God who is interdependent: "The disabled God is a God for whom interdependence is not a possibility to be willed from a position of power, but a necessary condition for life."[7] Here she proposes an interdependence that is more radical than those who define it as God's reliance on human agents to advance God's purpose in

---

[6]Mary Daly, *Beyond God the Father: Toward a Philosophy of Women's Liberation* (Boston: Beacon Press, 1985), 19.
[7]Eiesland, *Disabled God*, 103.

the world.[8] Eiesland says God does not simply will Godself to be "interrelated from a position of power" but experiences dependence "from a position of need."[9] She challenges us to move away from divinized abstractions of self-sufficiency and independence. She acknowledges that many will find her description of God unsettling, especially those "heavily invested in a belief in the transcendence of God constituted as radical otherness."[10] The transcendent God of most classical theism seems to be a god "whose attention we cannot get, whose inability to respond to our pain causes still more pain? This god is surely not Emmanuel—God for us."[11]

It is not surprising then, that vulnerability, as essential to human nature but also as an experience of God, is a common theme in theologies of disability, and is a concept that will be picked up in the chapters that follow. The picture of God painted by Eiesland above is of a God who is reached by our pain, for whom perfection does not mean a shelter from suffering, but an openness to real human experience, even to pain. Thomas Reynolds develops this theme in more detail than Eiesland in his book *Vulnerable Communion*. He describes God as vulnerable due to God's nature as love and because God created the universe as an open system with freedom. He draws primarily from Moltmann to indicate that God suffers with those God loves. "God is vulnerable to creation's interdependence; feeling pain and loss with creatures."[12] In Christ, God doesn't only suffer human vulnerability but also takes this into God's own being.[13]

A few theologies have highlighted a notion of God's interdependence with reference to the Trinity. They are worth mentioning here because of the attention that will be given to disability as it relates to the triune life of God in what follows.[14] Jennie Weiss Block's book *Copious Hosting: A Theology of Access for People with Disabilities* is primarily a guide for churches to

---

[8]An example of this approach is Kathy Black, *A Healing Homiletic: Preaching and Disability* (Nashville, TN: Abingdon Press, 1996).

[9]Eiesland, *Disabled God*, 103.

[10]Eiesland, *Disabled God*, 105.

[11]Eiesland, *Disabled God*, 105.

[12]Thomas E. Reynolds, *Vulnerable Communion: A Theology of Disability and Hospitality* (Grand Rapids, MI: Brazos Press, 2008), 166.

[13]Reynolds, *Vulnerable Communion*, 176–7.

[14]Theological ethicist Hans Reinders develops his anthropology with reference to God's triune life, drawing particularly from the social trinitariansim of John Zizioulas.

become more inclusive of people with disabilities, drawing from Catherine LaCugna's description of God's household as "a domain of inclusiveness, interdependence, and cooperation"[15] to argue that a theology of access "is built upon the three-part God." She says that "a life of love and communion with others where inclusion is the rule, not the exception, can only be realized in a Trinitarian context."[16] Similarly, *Discovering Trinity in Disability: A Theology for Embracing Difference* by Tataryn and Truchan-Tataryn develops a case for the inclusion of people with disabilities in the fullness of Christian community based upon the idea that the Trinity is constituted by relationship among the diverse persons of God. God is a community of difference, unified in love; thus, Christian parishes need to form communities of love, equality, and mutuality.

These examples follow the not-uncommon pattern of looking to the immanent life of God, and then drawing some conclusions about the way society or the Christian community should work together in light of this divine model.[17] The project developed in the chapters that follow will consider disability as it relates to God's triune life, but will take a different tack, endeavoring to avoid this "corrective projection," that is a type of trinitarian theology that identifies particular social/cultural values seen as oppressive or problematic, and then finds in the Trinity the solution to combat this value, such that the Trinity provides the model for the social structure or change the theologian seeks.[18] Though I will use analogies of relation to illustrate trinitarian relationships, conclusions about what the potentially disabled body of the Son means for humanity will rely not on projecting the Trinity into social systems but upon the Christian's engrafting into the impaired flesh of the incarnate One.

The approach developed in this book bears more in common with the brief trinitarian musings offered by Stanley Hauerwas in the "inconclusive theological postscript" to an influential essay published in 1986 on discourse around preventing intellectual

---

[15]Weiss Block quotes LaCugna directly here, *God for Us: The Trinity and Christian Life* (San Franciso: Harper Collins, 1993), 402.

[16]Jennie Weiss Block, *Copious Hosting: A Theology of Access for People with Disabilities* (New York: Continuum, 2002).

[17]Myroslaw Tataryn and Maria Truchan-Tataryn, *Discovering Trinity in Disability: A Theology for Embracing Difference* (Maryknoll, NY: Orbis Books, 2013), 63.

[18]I borrow this term from Linn Marie Tonstad, *God and Difference: The Trinity, Sexuality, and the Transformation of Finitude* (New York: Routledge, 2016).

disability.[19] There Hauerwas draws from Arthur McGill's account of the ancient Arian debate, arguing that the issue did not pertain to "whether God is one or two or three" but rather "what quality makes God divine, what quality constitutes his perfection."[20] He argues that while Arius identified God's perfection as "self-contained absoluteness and transcendent supremacy," Athanasius located God's perfection within "God's self-communicating love."[21] McGill claims that for Athanasius "Love and not transcendence, giving and not being superior, are qualities that mark God's divinity."[22] Thus McGill asserts that because "giving entails receiving, there must be a receptive, dependent, needy pole within the being of God. It is pride—and not love—that fears dependence and that worships transcendence."[23] If the marker of God's divinity as love includes the receptive, the dependent, and the needy, Hauerwas asserts that in the face of the intellectually disabled we are "offered an opportunity to see God, for like God they offer us an opportunity of recognizing the character of our neediness."[24] Using language now outdated for those with intellectual disability, Hauerwas writes:

The challenge of learning to know, to be with, and care for the retarded is nothing less than learning to know, be with, and love God. God's face is the face of the retarded; God's body is the body of the retarded; God's being is that of the retarded. For the God we Christians must learn to worship is not a god of self-sufficient power, a god who in self-possession needs no one; rather ours is a God who needs a people, who needs a son. Absoluteness of being or power is not a work of the God we have come to know through the cross of Christ.[25]

---

[19]Arthur McGill, *Suffering: A Test Case of Theological Method* (Philadelphia, PA: Westminster Press, 1983).

[20]Stanley Hauerwas, "Suffering the Retarded: Should We Prevent Retardation?," in *Critical Reflections on Stanley Hauerwas' Theology of Disability: Disabling Society, Enabling Theology*, ed. John Swinton. *Journal of Religion, Disability, and Health* 8 (3/4) (2004): 105; McGill, *Suffering*, 78.

[21]McGill, *Suffering*, 78, quoted by Hauerwas, "Suffering the Retarded," 105.

[22]McGill, *Suffering*, 78, quoted by Hauerwas, "Suffering the Retarded," 105.

[23]McGill, *Suffering*, 78, quoted by Hauerwas, "Suffering the Retarded," 105.

[24]Hauerwas, "Suffering the Retarded," 105.

[25]Hauerwas, "Suffering the Retarded," 104.

In this essay, Hauerwas seems to gesture particularly toward a need of the Father, as one needing a son.

I do not disagree that God constituted Godself to need "a people," in that God chose to determine God's being for the purpose of covenant. And I will argue that the Father also ventures a risk in this self-determining decision. However, in the theology I develop here, I will focus primarily on the Son as the mode of God's being that exists in a posture of receptivity, dependence, and need. Such experiences are not foreign to the being of God, but as I will argue throughout this book, are eternal to very triune being of God, not simply assumed in the moment of incarnation, but are aspects of the divine life from God's primordial self-determining decision.

Eiesland writes: "The disabled God embodies practical interdependence, not simply willing to be interrelated from a position of power, but depending on it from a position of need."[26] In what follows I will explore what it means for an interdependence to be a "necessary condition" for God's life by engaging an unlikely ally in the Trinitarian theology of Karl Barth. I utilize recent developments around divine ontology (conceptions of God's being) and protology (conceptions of the primordial, original being of God) in Barthian theology to lay the groundwork for a doctrine of God that takes embodiment seriously, emphasizes a deep connection between God and creation, and affirms the disabled body of God. Here God is three *because* God chose to be a God of creation, covenant, and incarnation. God's decision to exist in covenant relationship with creation is said to logically precede and ground God's self-determination as triune. God chose to be eternally enfleshed, limited, and weak, and we know no other God behind this decision.

Theological Ontology in Contemporary Barth Studies

Karl Barth's impact on theological method in the past century can hardly be overstated. His rule that all theological claims must be derived from God's self-revelation, though certainly not unique to Barth, was applied by him with particular rigor and influenced systematic theology across traditions, contributing to a shift away

---

[26]Eiesland, *Disabled God*, 103.

from speculation and metaphysics and a newly intensified focus on Jesus as God's revelation.[27] Theological anthropology comes from Christology—we know who we are as humans only because of who Jesus is. The doctrine of God, creation, pneumatology, and so on, are all derived from God's self-revelation, particularly in Jesus. God's self-revelation in history must truly be who God is within Godself, so there is no gap between the nature of God as revealed and the actual being of God within Godself. This means that while God is hidden in revelation, for example, the form of God hidden in Jesus, God is nonetheless truly revealed in Christ's life, death, and resurrection. In contrast, a God behind revelation that can't be known suggests a God who is possibly different from the one revealed and thus undercuts revelation itself: if God is different from who God is revealed to be, how can we trust that God is revealed in Christ at all, or that who Christ demonstrates God to be actually portrays the reality of the divine life? Thus, says Barth: "We have consistently followed the rule, which we regard as basic, that statements about the divine modes of being antecedently in themselves cannot be different in content from those that are to be made about their reality in revelation."[28]

We say that God is three persons (or three modes of being) because God has revealed Godself to be Father, Son, and Spirit in the economy of salvation; because of who God is revealed to be through God's dealings with creation and humanity, we come to know God as triune. How directly the economic trinity can be read into the reality of the immanent and eternal being of God is hotly debated in systematic theology. In recent Barth scholarship, however,

---

[27]Certainly many question Barth's method, which may discount the mystery of God's revelation and presence. It makes revelation seem as purely objective, as if Christ's life were a set of propositions to be read. The method actually moves away from a divinization of the biblical text, though, by refusing to equate the Bible with revelation. Of course, the intense focus on the incarnation of Jesus as revelation is also problematic for some theologians who pursue theologies open to pluralism and engaging in interreligious dialogue, as the focus on God in Christ as *the* revelation of God may be used to rule out the possibility of God being revealed in other ways and in other religious traditions. Theologians in his defense sometimes quote his statement that God can use a dead dog if God wants (*CD* I/1, p. 60): "God may speak to us through Russian communism, through a flute concerto, through a blossoming shrub or through a dead dog. We shall do well to listen to him if he really does so." See Karl Barth, *Church Dogmatics*, 4 volumes in 13 parts, ed. Thomas F. Torrance and Geoffrey W. Bromiley, trans. Geoffrey W. Bromiley (Edinburgh: T&T Clark, 1956–75).
[28]*CD* I/1, p. 479.

a debate likewise rages over how thoroughly Barth actually applied this principle in the development of his doctrine of God.

Those familiar with contemporary Barth studies in the United States are well aware of the heated exchanges among theologians over divine ontology and the relationship between the triunity of God and God's election. Many articles and essays have summarized the debate, and as this is not a book on the debate, nor even a book on Barth, I will not rehash the debate and intermediate positions, nor make a systematic defense of one interpretation. I will instead expound an understanding of God informed by these developments to advance the concerns raised by liberation theologies, specifically theologies of disability, and to reckon with the meaning and legacy of Eiesland's *Disabled God*.[29]

Perhaps some will be surprised that a debate in theological ontology in Barth studies would be of interest for liberation theology. The concerns raised in this controversy are primarily about the essence or being of God, seemingly far removed from the anthropological, sociological, and political concerns that feature more prominently in liberation theologies. How could such intricate detailing of the primordial ordering of the being of God have bearing on the pressing concerns of the oppressed in our world? An additional relevant concern is that this particular debate is fueled almost entirely by heterosexual, non-disabled, white male academics in the US context.

There are of course many reasons to critique Barth's theology generally. In some circles his name is nearly synonymous with sexism, heteronormativity, anti-Jewish supersessionism, and likely a handful of other disturbing oppressions related to various systematic theologies, conservatism, and the Christian tradition generally. He has been charged with proffering a docetic Christ, that is, of not reckoning with the humanity of Christ.[30] He is critiqued for his emphasis on the transcendence of God and the infinite qualitative distinction between God and creation, such that God seems very far off indeed. His theology has been accused of promoting oppressive social binaries and is also known for perpetuating

---

[29]Some of the ideas developed here can also be found in: Lisa D. Powell, "Disability and Covenant Ontology," in *Karl Barth and Liberation Theology*, ed. Kaitlyn Dugan and Paul Dafydd Jones (London: T&T Clark, 2023): 69–84.

[30]See James Cone, *God of the Oppressed*, revised edition (Maryknoll, NY: Orbis Press, 1997).

complementarianism and sexist stereotypes about gender roles and women's subordination.[31] And certainly some of his rhetoric is infamously virulent, as is that of some of his commentators.[32] So Barthian theology has earned a reputation of acrimony, some of which is certainly warranted, and I have no desire to justify him or his commentators when these charges are deserved. I certainly harbor some reservations as a feminist theologian to give positive attention to the theology of someone who remained committed to a complementarian, sexist, and heteronormative view of humanity. Yet the sweeping dismissal of his contributions in some circles has meant that those elements of his theology helpful to the cause of justice have also been neglected. I hope my work here will demonstrate a positive use for elements of Barth's thought for the purposes and commitments of liberation from a variety of perspectives and contexts.

I hope that by exploring the debate in theological ontology I may lay additional theological foundations for Eiesland's "disabled God" and extend her contribution to our understanding of the nature and being of God. I believe such an approach achieves many of the outcomes proposed by Eiesland. God stakes God's own being on relationship with creation, on the frailty of human form, on the gift-giving of those with whom God covenants; that is, God relies upon the creature not only for the completion of God's plan, but also for the fulfillment of the divine life itself, a fulfillment brought about in the incarnation and ascension of the impaired Christ into the eternal life of God.

The debate over divine ontology in Barth studies ignited with the publication of Bruce McCormack's essay "Grace and Being" in *The Cambridge Companion to Karl Barth*.[33] A passionate barrage

---

[31]This concern of social hierarchies and how Barth theologically grounds inequality is a difficult case. I will not defend his position, but in the following chapters I will offer some hope for an alternative interpretation and language for the Father–Son relationship, which is the theological starting point for some of his claims about male and female relationships.

[32]Tillich called Barth's writing "a demonic absolutism which throws the truth like stones at the heads of people not caring whether they can accept it or not." Quoted by John Webster, "Introducing Barth," in *The Cambridge Companion to Karl Barth*, ed. John Webster (Cambridge: Cambridge University Press, 2000), 9.

[33]Bruce McCormack, "Grace and Being: The Role of God's Gracious Election in Karl Barth's Theological Ontology," in *The Cambridge Companion to Karl Barth*, ed. John Webster (Cambridge: Cambridge University Press, 2000), 92–110.

of publications followed: some repudiating McCormack's position, others defending it, and others attempting to mediate.[34] Of course, McCormack also contributed, with continued clarifications and developments of his position, culminating most recently with the publication of the first volume of his constructive theology inspired by some of the Barthian insights first laid out in the controversial essay.

A significant portion of the scholarship around this debate pertains to whether or not a real shift occurred in Barth's thinking, whether he was inconsistent, and whether he would agree with the ontology proposed by McCormack as rooted in Barth's own suggestions. The debate often centers on who is the more accurate interpreter and faithful reader of Barth.[35] I am not interested, however, in how Barth would react to this reading or to my application of it here. Nor am I interested in delineating who is the better expositor of Barth and his intentions. Quite simply I find the position developed by McCormack, and others who prioritize election to Trinity, to make the most theological sense and to resonate with theologies committed to justice and liberation.

A key point in the debate is the question of whether God self-determines as triune, or whether subsistence as triune is necessary to God; or, put differently, whether Barth's remarks about divine self-determination refer to God's decision to *constitute* Godself as the triune God, or whether such remarks are simply a way of identifying God as the God of creation and covenant. McCormack favors the former position: God self-determines God's eternal being, which makes triunity a logical "consequence" of God's decision to be a God of covenant. Obviously the language here is tricky; there is no real "before" with respect to God's triunity. Yet we can still speak of an origin or that which is logically "prior," and that which founded what follows, much as one might say the Father is "prior"

---

[34]A collection of articles central to the debate, and a few additional essays related, are gathered by Michael T. Dempsey, ed. in *Trinity and Election in Contemporary Theology* (Grand Rapids, MI: Eerdmans, 2011). Dempsey's introduction to the volume also provides a good summary of the development of the debate; see pp. 1–25.
[35]See for example George Hunsinger's book-length rebuttal, *Reading Barth with Charity: A Hermeneutical Proposal* (Grand Rapids, MI: Baker Academic, 2015). Some of the "revisionist" camp (the name Hunsinger and others give to those who read a prioritization of election to trinity in later Barth) acknowledge that they are straying some from Barth, and McCormack openly acknowledges that his ongoing work is his own constructive project in light of these ideas found in Barth's work.

as the origin of Son and Spirit, and yet all three simultaneously exist as the eternal God. So, then, what is prior? God's existence as three "persons," or God's existence as directed to the covenant of grace?[36]

Most traditional theologies take God's triunity as a "given," not as a result of a self-determining decision. God's triune identity as Father, Son, and Spirit in loving union is essential to God, original, and "prior" to God's decision to enter into covenant relationship outside Godself.[37] That is to say: God exists in interpenetrating, abundant love "before" God determines Godself to be a God of covenant. God's triune nature grounds God's decision to create and be a God of relationship with something other than Godself. At times, however, Barth's references to God's self-determination seem to point back not only to God's self-determination to be God-for-us, but also God's initial primordial determination of God's very being as triune.

Before *Church Dogmatics* II/2 (*CD* II/2), Barth affirms triunity as logically prior to election, with statements like:

God would be no less God if He had created no world and no human being. The existence of the world and our existence are in no sense vital to God, not even as the object of His love. The eternal generation of the Son by the Father tells us first and supremely that God is not at all lonely even without the world and us. His love has its object in Himself.[38]

These statements correspond well with the tradition, and with the image of God as utterly independent of the world, existing in

---

[36]Though in early publications McCormack seemed to give ontological priority to election, he has since indicated that he is only speaking of a logical priority—this is one act with two terms.

[37]Those in the debate who oppose the priority of election will say triunity is "necessary" to God as a way to establish with clarity that triunity is in no way conditioned by God's decision. God does not self-determine as triune; there is no way to speak of a "before" this reality, not even logically. This is also a way opponents contrast their necessity of triunity to what they deem a necessity of creation in theological projects that prioritize election logically to triunity. See for example Paul Molnar, *Divine Freedom and the Doctrine of the Immanent Trinity: In Dialogue with Karl Barth and Contemporary Theology, 2nd Edition* (London: T&T Clark, 2017), 153.

[38]*CD* I/1, pp. 139–40.

perfect triune love without the world. If we take Barth's idea of revelation as *self*-revelation seriously, however, we may find a gap between this triune God who loves Godself in utter freedom and the decision to then determine God's being for incarnation and covenant. McCormack sees a move in Barth to close this gap. "Talk of an 'ontological priority' of Trinity over election must inevitably result in an abstract, wholly metaphysical conception of the triune being of God that stands behind the event in which God chooses to be God 'for us' in Jesus Christ."[39] And here is where Barth did not seem to follow his method through to its conclusion.

In *Church Dogmatics* II/2 and subsequent part-volumes, however, Barth's talk of the being of God suggests a different way of thinking about God's triune existence. Barth opens the door to understand God's triunity as the *consequence* of God's eternal self-determination to be a God of covenant. God constitutes God's being as triune in God's gracious electing decision. Here God's free decision to be in covenant relationship with that which is not God determines God's triune identity, which means that God's very eternal being is primordially shaped by this "prior" decision. God is triune for the purpose of relationship with that which is other than God. Or, as McCormack puts it in "Grace and Being": "God is triune *for the sake* of his revelation."[40] God's eternal being is "knowable because it is constituted by the act of turning toward us."[41] Thus, the gap of knowing God before or behind the God of revelation shrinks in size, if not closes entirely.

McCormack labels this "covenant ontology."[42] It is common to hear about a relational ontology, pointing simply to the idea that God's existence *is* God's internal relationship: God subsists in relationship. Then this God of relationship and love wants to share this love outside Godself and so God determines to create. In contrast covenant ontology understands God's being to be grounded

---

[39]Bruce McCormack, "Election and Trinity: Thesis in Response to George Hunsinger," in *Trinity and Election in Contemporary Theology*, ed. Michael T. Dempsey (Grand Rapids, MI: Eerdmans, 2011), 119.

[40]McCormack, "Grace and Being," 101.

[41]McCormack, "Grace and Being," 99.

[42]As these ideas took shape over subsequent years in McCormack's own constructive theological project, he has preferred to speak of a "psychological ontology." See Alexandra Pârvan and Bruce L. McCormack, "Immutability, (Im)possibility, and Suffering: Steps toward a "Psychological" Ontology of God," *Neue Zeitschrift für Systematische Theologie und Relgionsphilosophie* 59 (1) (2017): 1–25.

not "first" in internal relationships but directed toward covenant relationship, thus resulting in internal relationships. God's triune identity does not "precede" God's decision to be God with what is other than God. God is not relational simply within Godself prior to God's decision to be in relationship in this concrete, particular way. As Barth says, "God Himself does not will to be God, and is not God, except as the one who elects."[43]

At the center of this understanding of God's self-determination is Barth's Christology. Tradition locates Jesus within the economic Trinity, within the context of God revealing Godself in time, but not in God's primordial life. The Son, yes; Jesus, not yet.[44] Nonetheless, Barth makes a mysterious claim that stands at the heart of this splintering divide in Barth studies: "Jesus Christ is the electing God ... In no depth of the Godhead shall we encounter any but Him."[45] He insists that it is Jesus who is the subject of election, *is* the electing God, not the Logos or eternal Son, but specifically Jesus Christ. He says there is no "godhead in itself ... there is no such thing as a will of God apart from the will of Jesus Christ."[46] The "godhead" has always been determined by the becoming of Jesus Christ. McCormack summarizes the position well when he says simply: "The second 'person' of the Trinity has a name and [that] name is Jesus Christ."[47]

How does one make sense of this? How can the historical, embodied human being be present in the primordial being of God? How can it be asserted that Jesus *is* the second mode of God's being, if Jesus comes into being specifically at a point in time, as all humans do? Certainly Mary's genetic material did not preexist.[48]

---

[43]*CD* II/2, p. 77.

[44]One notable exception here could be Origen, yet his theology did not remain influential in the formation of Western theology. In fact some have charged that McCormack's and similar positions are an example of the resurgence of heretical Origenism. See Paul Molnar, *Faith, Freedom, and the Spirit: The Economic Trinity in Barth, Torrence, and Contemporary Theology* (Downers Grove, IL: InterVarsity Press, 2015), 187–224.

[45]*CD* II/2, p. 115.

[46]*CD* II/2, p. 115.

[47]McCormack, "Grace and Being," 100.

[48]Robert Jenson, in his rejection of the concept of *logos asarkos*, names well this conundrum for the mind shaped by Western philosophy and expectations of linearity. "That Mary is *Theotokos* indeed disrupts the linear time-line or pseudo time-line on which we Westerners automatically—and usually subliminally—locate every event,

Yet this position insists that the eternal Logos is Jesus Christ, the God-human, who is Jesus of Nazareth, born of a humble young Jewish woman, her true genetic offspring; Mary is *Theotokos*, the God-bearer. Robert Jenson explains, "In whatever way the Son may antecede his conception by Mary, we must not posit the Son's antecedent subsistence in such fashion as to make the incarnation the addition of the human Jesus to a Son who was himself without him."[49] Similarly for Barth, the God-human, Jesus Christ, is present eternally as the Son by way of anticipation because of the electing decision that shapes the eternal divine life. The second mode of God's being is proleptically, though eternally, determined by the history of Jesus. Barth writes, "According to the free and gracious will of God the eternal Son of God is Jesus Christ as he lived and died and rose again in time, and none other."[50] There is no other subsistence to the Son behind this history. "Any talk of the eternal Son in abstraction from the humanity to be assumed is an exercise in mythologizing; there is no such eternal Son—and there never was."[51] It is Jesus *in all his history* who is the preexistent God for us.

Those who hold this position give a significantly limited role to the *logos asarkos,* the word without flesh, or deny the concept altogether. There is no Logos behind the decision to become incarnate, and so McCormack speaks of the name Logos as a "placeholder" for the proper name for God's second "person," which is Jesus Christ. The incarnation and history of Jesus is constitutive of the identity of the second person of the Trinity, without metaphysical remainder outside of, or behind, the real person of Jesus. We proleptically identify Jesus Christ as the second person of the eternal triune life of God, a full identification of the second mode of God's being with Jesus Christ in his human history. At minimum this would mean that Jesus is there at the beginning of time, something Barth affirms in *CD* II/2: "He, Jesus, in the beginning, is with God, is by nature God. That is what is being secured in John 1:1."[52] McCormack

---

even the birth of God the Son." "Once More the *Logos Asarkos,*" *International Journal of Systematic Theology* 13 (1) (2011): 131.

[49]Jenson, "Once More the *Logos Asarkos,*" 130.

[50]*CD* IV/1, p. 52; see also *CD* III/2, p. 66; Darren O. Sumner, *Karl Barth and the Incarnation: Christology and the Humility of* God (New York: T&T Clark, 2016), 104.

[51]Bruce L. McCormack, "The Actuality of God: Karl Barth in Conversation with Open Theism," in *Engaging the Doctrine of God: Contemporary Protestant Perspectives* (Grand Rapids, MI: Baker Academic, 2008), 218–19.

[52]*CD* II/2, p. 96.

summarizes: "That Jesus has his being in the Logos *eternally* can mean only that the Logos is never without Jesus and that therefore God is a human God."[53]

The tradition has reserved the term *logos asarkos* to refer to the Son in the immanent life of God before the incarnation as the full divine-human subject of Jesus. It also preserves the idea that the being of the Son is not exhausted in this unity; the Son is not confined to the human body of Jesus but continues to "fill all things."[54] *Logos asarkos* corresponds with the image of God upheld by most tradition as the God of unfettered autonomy in perfect contentment within Godself, who then decides to create and to become a human being among creation either because humanity went awry and the God-human could fix it, or because God intended to become incarnate for purposes of revelation. One can see how this understanding of *logos asarkos* helps preserve an image of a transcendent God, independent of creation and without need. Covenant ontology has no need for this concept in distinction from the God-human unity of Jesus Christ.

For the ancients the human body itself posed problems for divinity. The body is essentially mutable. The whole of human existence is a movement of growth and then decline to decay. The body is a vehicle for the passions—pleasure and pain—both of which are problematic for the divine stasis of contentment. The human experience of the incarnate One has always caused difficulty for theologians committed to divine immutability. God's being is eternal; God does not experience change, but to be human is to endure change. The incarnation jeopardizes precommitments to immutability, impassibility, and transcendence, and it threatens to introduce in God weakness, vulnerability, and dependence. Thus it's no wonder theologians have hotly, and even violently, debated explanations of the hypostatic union for centuries. The concept of *logos asarkos* suggests that the humanity of Jesus is not rightly attributable to the divine being. The second mode of God's being is not determined by the incarnation, but stands behind it whole and complete, and would have remained the same in being and

---

[53]Bruce L. McCormack, "Participation in God: Yes; Deification, No: Two Modern Protestant Responses to an Ancient Question," in *Orthodox and Modern: Studies in the Theology of Karl Barth* (Grand Rapids, MI: Baker Academic, 2008), 246.

[54]Eph. 4:10 Beyond this, further debate persists as to whether one can speak of a *logos asarkos* and the *logos incarnatus* simultaneously. Does the Logos have an identity that is more than or different from the intention for incarnation?

content had God decided not to create or becoming incarnate. This understanding of the eternal identity of the Son works to preserve the immutability and impassability of God.

Although many liberation theologies surrender immutability for the sake of a passible God, a God who truly experiences human suffering in Christ, a covenant ontology retains a commitment to divine immutability, while abandoning the expected associated attribute: impassibility. Many contemporary theologians are more than comfortable accepting change as compatible with God's being and life; this is central to process theology and open theism for example. Yet other theologians hold to a doctrine of divine immutability as assurance of God's faithfulness and the veracity of revelation as the true disclosure of God's constancy and eternal being. Justo Gonzales explains the position differently, but it resonates with the position developed here: "if there is any sense in which the God of the Bible can be described as 'immutable,' this has nothing to do with impassibility or ontological immobility, but rather with the assurance that God's 'steadfast love endureth forever.' "[55] Because God is eternally constituted for the assumption of humanity as God's own body and history and for the introduction of real human experience as God's second mode of being, the incarnation does not introduce change into God's being; God's essence doesn't alter in order to experience real human suffering. As McCormack explains,

> If becoming human, suffering, and dying, and so forth, are the content of the eternal decision in which God gives himself his being, then no change is introduced into the being of God when this becoming and so forth takes place in time. And if God is immutably determined for suffering, then the concept of immutability has been cut loose from impassibility.[56]

In addition to divine impassibility, covenant ontology departs from a traditional preservation of divine simplicity. God has determined Godself to be complicated in God's second mode of being. Either God changes, or somehow a composite God-human person is also the second person of the eternal Trinity, and the way to explain that, without imputing change into God, is to understand God's being

---

[55]Justo L. Gonzales, *Mañana: Christian Theology from a Hispanic Perspective* (Nashville, TN: Abingdon Press, 1990), 92.
[56]Bruce McCormack, "The Actuality of God," 223.

as always directed toward this incarnate life. God truly experiences human development and suffering in the God-human unity that is Jesus Christ. God's self-constitution for covenant, means that God chooses even a complication of God's being. McCormack explains:

> The "person" is made to be composite not through adding something to a divine being that is complete in itself without reference to the human. No, the second "person" of the Trinity is himself "composite"; in himself he already is, by way of anticipation (as founded in election), what he will become in time .... Thus "Jesus Christ" (i.e. the God-human in his divine-human unity) is the identity of the second "person" of the Trinity—not only in time but also "in himself" (when, as yet, there was no creation standing in need of redemption). ... There is no "person" somehow "beneath" the two natures as that in which they "subsist." The two "natures"—really, divine and human *being*—are made one in a single human history.[57]

God chooses to be ontologically complex, as Paul Dafydd Jones explains: this is "a love that goes to extreme lengths—a love that stops at nothing, not even the complication of God's being—to realize companionship with humanity."[58]

The traditional position certainly affirms that triunity precedes God's electing decision for covenant, and defenders of this position believe that this affirmation is essential to protect the freedom of God.[59] Since God is eternally self-sufficient, talk of the priority of election is unacceptable; it postulates an eternal God as "needing" that which is not God, an eternal God who is originally not self-sufficient. Aaron Smith describes the traditional view of God thus: "there is that eternity in which God is in himself, as he exists in triune seclusion, utterly free and not contingent, able to assign himself his being with recourse to none but himself, happily alone in unfettered autonomy and perfect contentment apart from all that

---

[57]McCormack, "The Person of Christ," in *Mapping Modern Theology: A Thematic and Historical Introduction*, ed. Kelly M. Kapic and Bruce L. McCormack (Grand Rapids, MI: Baker Academic, 2012), 171.

[58]Paul Dafydd Jones, *The Humanity of Christ: Christology in Karl Barth's Church Dogmatics* (London: T&T Clark, 2008), 213.

[59]Critics will also charge that because this ontology makes creation in some sense necessary for the fulfillment of God's being that creation is no longer an act of grace.

is not he."[60] This is an image with which most readers of liberation theology are familiar as that depiction of God common to the tradition and fiercely critiqued from a wide variety of perspectives and contexts: feminist, postcolonial, queer, Black theology, and so on. In a covenant ontology, by contrast, God's eternal being is bound to creation not just through a "subsequent" decision to create and covenant with Israel; God is bound to creation in the very founding of God's triune eternal being. If God determines God's being for the sake of revelation, and creation is necessary for revelation, then God "needs" creation. And if God in God's second way of being is begotten for the purpose of incarnation, God needs humanity, needs fulfillment in the hypostatic union. If the "second person" of the Trinity is truly Jesus Christ, then surely it is accurate to say God's eternal being is always directed to incarnation; this is the founding decision that results in the tri-ordered life of God—one directed to creation, incarnation, and Pentecost. This could be a win for liberation theologies seeking to stress Jesus' ministry with the poor and the marginalized as truly indicative of God's nature; the full history of Jesus' life and mission is who God is in God's second mode.

Most theologians would be comfortable saying that creation is a precondition of the self-communication of God's triune life—that creation is "necessary" for revelation. But we are saying something much more here, and this additional layer of meaning is what stirs great anxiety among Barth scholars who, for various reasons, seek to affiliate Barth with the tradition. God self-determines to be triune in anticipation of fellowship with creation. Because the intention for creation is the precondition of God's self-determination, it would seem to make creation not only necessary for God's self-revelation but also for the fulfillment of God's very being. God is never "unfettered"; deep within God's eternal being, God needs—God needs the recipient of covenant relationship, and the Son needs the humanity of Jesus (and thus embodiment) to fulfill and complete the Son's identity as the God-human. McCormack does not shirk from acknowledging the necessity this perspective places on creation for the being of God: "Given the divine will to redeem, creation was made 'necessary'; God had to become the Creator. There exists

---

[60]Aaron T. Smith, "God's Self-Specification: His Being Is His Electing," in *Trinity and Election in Contemporary Theology*, 217.

an 'ontic connection'; between Jesus Christ and creation."[61] The cosmos, then, is not an add-on to a self-sufficient God who existed in primordial loving relation within God's own life. Rather, God's very immanent life is determined to be for this cosmos to such a degree that God determines to be triune for the purpose of this relationship. Not vice versa. God is not triune and then makes use of that triunity to enable revelation and the economy of salvation. God self-constitutes as triune in order to be in covenant and to embrace that creation within God's very being. Barth even declares that in this electing decision, God determines not to be "entirely self-sufficient."[62] In response to this quotation from Barth, Kevin Hector voices the terror many Christians may feel over such a thought: "God—not self-sufficient? From eternity?!"[63]

Covenant Ontology and Disability

We now move to the ways this account of the originating decision of triunity for the sake of covenant is promising for disability theology and perhaps other theologies of liberation, and will be foundational for the argument I develop throughout this book. It may not be a surprise that many of the most promising implications of this account are exactly the points most targeted by critics who wish to preserve elements of "classical theism" (which is a perspective that many liberation theologians reject or reconfigure):[64] (1) It introduces "need" into the being of God; (2) it establishes an ontological

---

[61]Bruce L. McCormack, "The Identity of the Son: Karl Barth's Exegesis of Hebrews 1:1-4 (and Similar Passages)," in *Christology, Hermeneutics, and Hebrews: Profiles from the History of Interpretation*, ed. Jon C. Laansma and Daniel J. Treier (New York: T&T Clark, 2012), 170, quoting *CD* III/1, pp. 49, 58, and 51. McCormack qualifies this somewhat in other publications, calling it a "contingent necessity."

[62]*CD* II/2, p. 10.

[63]Kevin W. Hector, "God's Triunity and Self-Determination: A Conversation with Karl Barth, Bruce McCormack, and Paul Molnar," in *Trinity and Election in Contemporary Theology*, 42.

[64]See for example Karen Baker Fletcher, *Dancing with God: The Trinity from a Womanist Perspective* (St. Louis, MO: Chalice Press, 2007), Mayra Rivera, *The Touch of Transcendence: A Postcolonial Theology of God* (Louisville, KY: Westminster John Knox Press, 2007), Katherine Keller, *Face of the Deep: A Theology of Becoming* (New York: Routledge, 2003), Elizabeth Johnson, *Quest for the Living God: Mapping Frontiers in the Theology of God* (New York: Continuum 2007).

connection between God and the cosmos—not just by a decision to relate, but a connection that is eternal and necessary to God's second way of being; (3) it positions God as vulnerable, since God risks the "fulfillment" or "completion" of divine life in the humanity of Jesus; (4) it makes humanity and embodiment necessary to the being of God; (5) it posits a posture of ontological receptivity for the Son, or an interdependence within the being of God, beyond a perichoretic interdependence of the trinitarian "persons."

The promise for liberation theologies here should be apparent. Numerous theologies critique the classic portrayals of God that suggest a solitary independent power, whose very nature is autonomous self-sufficiency. Such a God is not acceptable to theologians who want to combat the images of ideal humanity as independent, perfectly capable/able in all things alone. Too often this sociocultural value for humanity is projected with superlative status to God. Moreover, such an image of God does not comport with God's revelation in Jesus. Liberation theologians charge that this God of transcendence and omnipotence divinizes worldly, masculinist power, and portrays God more as a tyrant than as the One who enters into marginalized human existence as a poor Jew, ushers in a reign of justice for the poor and oppressed, and endures persecution and execution by the Empire. Yet a covenant ontology not only suggests that God is not self-sufficient because of the incarnation, because Jesus needed Mary to care for him, for example, but infinitely more, God is not self-sufficient within Godself from all eternity. Such a value of self-sufficiency has no place in God whatsoever; undercutting the very social elevation of independence as virtue.

All of this, then, allows a pair of summary claims. (1) God is not, in essence, autonomous. Aaron Smith put it this way: "The reality that Jesus Christ is the subject of election precludes the possibility of ... eternal autonomy, since in this event, as this event, a nonautonomous deity is fully revealed."[65] (2) If Jesus truly is identified as the second person of the Trinity, humanity is not foreign to the being of God; humanity can even be said to be constitutive of the life of God in God's second mode. Darren Sumner says, "What seems to us a contradiction—that a created essence is made essential to the Creator—is maintained by the freedom of God."[66] Embodiment and

---

[65]Aaron T. Smith, "God's Self-Specification: His Being Is His Electing," 225.
[66]Sumner, *Karl Barth and the Incarnation*, 204.

humanity become essential to the being of God, and this is a massive departure from the account of God often critiqued by liberation theology. Here, embodiment does not just exist as part of God at a point in time via incarnation; embodiment, rather, is essential to God's being from all eternity because of the original act of God's self-determination to be the triune God for the sake of covenant.

Logos incarnandus fractus

A number of people in this debate consider what the eventual suffering of Jesus means for this eternal identity of the Son. Paul Dafydd Jones writes, "God qua Son is never not humanized; God *qua* Son is never not the Christ who undergoes suffering."[67] Barth himself writes:

> The New Testament describes the Son of God ... not only as the servant, but rather as the *suffering* servant of God. Not accidentally and provisionally does He *also* suffer—perhaps to the end of testing and preserving His basic conviction, perhaps for the attainment of a concrete goal through struggle, perhaps as a foil for emphasizing His glory in another way, but necessarily and to a certain extent, essentially.[68]

McCormack comments: "On Barthian soil, the statement that God is 'essentially' a suffering God is not an abstract metaphysical assertion. It is a concrete affirmation of a concrete reality—Jesus Christ as the One who suffers in time is what God is 'essentially'."[69] However, what Barth and multiple commentators recognize but fail to name, is that God as Son is at essence, from God's primordial self-determination, the *disabled* God. God as Son is never not the disabled Christ because God determined to be shaped eternally by and for the history of Jesus, one who is wounded, impaired, and also as will be argued in the next chapter, as the Son is constituted for receptivity.

[67]Jones, *The Humanity of Christ*, 148–9.
[68]Quoted by Bruce L. McCormack, "Karl Barth's Historicized Christology: Just How 'Chalcedonian' Is It?," in *Orthodox and Modern: Studies in the Theology of Karl Barth* (Grand Rapids, MI: Baker Academic, 2008), 216. (CD IV/1: 164).
[69]McCormack, "Karl Barth's Historicized Christology," 218.

We regularly read accounts of the suffering of Christ and the suffering of God, but it remains somewhat vague and abstract—just "suffering." What Eiesland's bold identification of a disabled God accomplishes, among other things, is to remind us that this suffering is a particular suffering body, and although the suffering of Christ is not limited to his bodily suffering, it is in part the very impairment of his body to which we are referring when we speak of Christ's suffering or passion. Moreover, as disability literature stresses, the suffering of people with disabilities is not limited to physical pain or struggle; it is also tied up with social stigma, lack of access, social barriers, and dehumanization. The *logos incarnandus*, the Word to be in flesh, then is specifically the Logos anticipating the assumption of *broken* flesh, and a body that is outcast, rejected, and persecuted by social, religious, and political institutions. This, in the final analysis, is specifically who the Logos *is*; and this is the original free decision of God's self-determination and constitution: to be a human on the fringe, a human stigmatized, who suffers in the body, and who suffers the psychological and emotional pain of rejection and isolation. So it is the real suffering of Jesus, the disabled God, that is central to the very nature of the Christian faith. This is the flesh anticipated from eternity. It is not just that Jesus retained a broken body, so that the humanity of God is ever after a wounded, enfleshed humanity. Jesus is the Lamb that was slain from the foundation of the world. God in God's second way of being has always been anticipating a disabled body. The eternal primal identity of the Son is not the *logos asarkos*, and is not even the *logos incarnandus*, but more specifically is the *logos incarnandus fractus* (the word going to be in broken flesh).[70]

This disabled body is not the only aspect of humanity anticipated of course. We are not only our bodies, but our bodies are certainly essential to our humanity. God became identified with humanity in becoming Jesus Christ, and this includes a creatureliness, a connection to the whole cosmos, a body with material origins in the stardust like the rest of the planet, like the universe. Thus we can speak of "God's existence as creature."[71] One can say God is bound

---

[70]I am grateful to my colleague and friend Fr. Bud Grant for helping me with the Latin needed to describe the eternally anticipated, impaired, and stigmatized humanity of Jesus.

[71]Eberhard Jüngel, *God's Being Is in His Becoming: The Trinitarian Being of God in the Theology of Karl Barth*, trans. John Webster (London: T&T Clark, 2014), 98.

to creation, not only because God determined to be God for us, but even more because God's very eternal being is primordially shaped by this "prior" decision. Barth warns that we ought not try to "limit in any way the solidarity with the cosmos which God accepted in Jesus Christ."[72] God hazards God's being on this venture, to establish God's self as so bound to the cosmos, that God's identity is shaped by and for this relationship. God takes creatureliness as God's own, as not foreign to the life and being of God, but true to the eternal existence and identity of God in God's second mode. This is specifically who the Logos is, this is the original free decision of God's self-determination and constitution: to be a human on the margins, a human fully identified with those whose bodies are broken, stigmatized, and persecuted. No Logos stands behind this history, immune, protected, or different from this Jesus Christ.

---

[72]CD IV/1, p. 215.

3

The Vulnerability and Need of God

One of the perennial challenges in Christian theology is how to explain the relationship between the human and the divine natures within the single subject who is Jesus Christ because the two natures are considered totally incompatible. The church's original responses to this puzzle were shaped in part by a conception of God's perfection that required that the divine nature be protected in some sense from a humanity that would, to their understanding, compromise it through the mutability of the human of the union. The underlying conviction involves an assumption that God's way of being and that of humanity are "not merely different but also logically irreconcilable. It is unthinkable that God should be affected by physical conditions of any sort or that [God] should share in human emotion or human ignorance."[1] But we see all of this in Jesus. He was born and grew in wisdom and in stature (Lk. 2:52), he seemed ignorant of knowledge held by the Father (Mt. 24:36, Mk 13:32), he appears to be making real and difficult decisions in his temptation in the wilderness (Mk 1:12) and under great stress in the Garden before his arrest (Lk. 22:44). And of course, most obviously, he suffered and died.

Two prominent approaches emerged that dealt with the complication differently. One associated with Antioch and the Bishop Nestorius suggests that the divine and the human in Christ can be precisely distinguished, such that one can point to exactly

---

[1]Richard A. Norris Jr., "Introduction," in *Christological Controversy* (Minneapolis, MN: Fortress Press, 1980), 20.

what moment in Jesus' life the divine is at work, and what moment it is his humanity. Here one assumes the ability to tease out flashes of divinity (miracles, "I am" statements, particular knowledge) from the abasements of humanity (surrender, suffering, and lack of knowledge). The unity of the one subject in this instance is at best merely logical. Alternatively, the Christology associated with Alexandria preserves the union of the subject by downplaying the fullness of the human nature, without denying its reality outright. Though the Council of Chalcedon (451) is typically taught as a mediating decision between the two, most theologians familiar with the results of this and subsequent councils recognize the persisting influence of the Alexandrian interpretation of Christ in the centuries that followed.

In order to emphasize the union of these two distinct natures, the church spoke of a communication of properties (*communicatio idiomatum*) whereby they claimed one could appropriately predicate attributes of each nature to the other on the basis of this union; however, when this was actually applied, it was the divine attributes at work on or in the human, but never the human attributes applied truly to the divine nature. Sarah Coakley notes that "none of the patristic authors ... argued that *human* attributes could be directly attributed to the divine nature."[2] In order to account for the biblical witness of Jesus' humanity and the divine-human union, Cyril of Alexandria explained that Christ "at 'times'... '*permitted* his own flesh to experience its proper affections'; but this was a 'permission' operated all along, it seems, from the unshakeable base of the Logos' unchanging divinity."[3] By the eighth century, according to Coakley, the *communicatio idiomatum* was "explicitly said to operate only *one way* (from the divine to the human), the divine fully permeating the human nature of Christ by an act of 'coinherence.'"[4] With orthodoxy strictly committed to principles of immutability and impassibility, the thought of human attributes impacting the divine in any authentic way was out of bounds.

---

[2]Sarah Coakley, *Powers and Submissions: Spirituality, Philosophy, and Gender* (Oxford: Wiley-Blackwell, 2002), 14.
[3]Coakley, *Powers and Submissions*, 15, quoting Cyril *De recta fide* II.55 (Coakley's emphasis).
[4]Coakley. *Powers and Submissions*, 15.

Thus, theologians since antiquity have typically understood Jesus' submission to the Father to be an expression of Jesus' humanity and a reflection neither of the divine nature of Christ, nor of the Son's relationship to the Father, which as consubstantial is not subordinated. Such submission or obedience would not be reflected back upon the divine nature. The agency within Christ is singularly divine, and the *communicatio idiomatum* is exclusively unidirectional. Jesus' humanity surrenders to God, but this should not suggest that the Son exists eternally in a posture of submission to the Father. To say otherwise, for most theologians, would mean a subordinationist account of the Trinity, that is: heresy.

This pull to sublimate the human to the divine in Christ and to preserve the divine unaffected by the union created a lasting and formative influence on the shape Christology could take within the bounds of orthodoxy for centuries. The unity of the subject of Jesus has thus been preserved by conceding only the divine as active within him, with possibly a few moments where the divine gives the human permission for expression of some human trait of ignorance or fatigue, while the human nature exists in perpetual receptivity of this divine action, or unceasing submission to the divine agency within the union that is Jesus Christ. Thus tradition has leaned toward a rather docetic conception of this relationship, such that the divine is the absolute active agent utilizing the humanity as a tool or instrument.

The resulting portrait of Jesus is unsatisfactory, if not disturbing, as the real humanity becomes negligible, functioning more as equipment for use by the Logos. Such a view of the human nature does not stand up to the standard requirement laid out by Gregory of Nazianzus: what is not assumed is not healed. If the humanity of Jesus is described like a puppet of flesh inhabited by the Logos in order to orchestrate salvation, then it is not a true humanity at all, which must have a will and a mind in addition to flesh and bones, and of course this debate over the mind and will of Christ raged for centuries beyond Chalcedon. Yet, even among those who strove to affirm a full humanity, it was typically a humanity dominated and controlled by the overwhelming force of the divinity with which it is united.

Clearly these approaches would not cohere with the theology developed in this book, where the experience of Jesus' humanity is taken into the life of God with such intention that the Trinity is shaped for this very purpose. And in fact, McCormack, in abandoning immutability and simplicity, explicitly admits that this ontology "renders the being of God affective."[5] God can be acted upon because of God's self-determination to be truly human in the God-human unity of God's second mode of being. According to this account the Son is ontologically receptive, eternally determined to receive the experience of humanity into God's life. This could be a win for liberation theologies that want to stress God's solidarity with the oppressed and marginalized. The full human life and experience of Jesus is truly an experience of God's own life; God is not kept at a distance from humanity and creation, but God determines Godself to be authentically impacted by human life.

One can argue for this eternal receptivity of the Son based on the eternal processions of the Trinity, that is, the Son receives personhood through the generating agency of the Father, so that the Son is begotten, and the Spirit receives personhood (in typical Western theology) from Father and Son, that is the Spirit spirates from both. The identities of the triune "persons" are established through these relations, sometimes referred to as relations of origin; thus these "persons" are shaped by initiating the personhood of another and/or by the reception of personhood. This difference in origin, generation, and procession accounts for the distinction of "persons." All are one God, but each is distinct from the other as a result of their differing relations: the Father as the origin, the Son as the one begotten from the Father, and the Spirit as the one breathed forth from Father and Son.

These eternal processions (being generated as Son or being breathed as Spirit) are then said to be revealed through the missions (or the sendings) of Son and Spirit in time. The Father as origin of Son and Spirit (together with the Son) is not sent but sends. This translates to the accounts of some theologians, Barth among them, of the Father as the one who commands. When Barth applies his strict rule of revelation in Jesus to the identities of Father and Son, he sees the obedience of Jesus as revelatory of the obedience of the eternal Son to the Father within the triune life of God. The Son as begotten and sent translates to a Son who obeys and follows. The Father as origin is one who commands and leads.

---

[5]Bruce L. McCormack, *The Humility of the Eternal Son: Reformed Kenoticism and the Repair of Chalcedon* (Cambridge: Cambridge University Press, 2021), 258.

Kenotic Christology

The historical Christological options discussed thus far don't make sense within a covenant ontology. Though the Son is understood as begotten of the Father, which establishes the distinct personhood of the Son, this receptivity does not extend to the identity of the Son as revealed in Jesus. According to traditional accounts, in the incarnation the Son transitions from a posture of begottenness (or of receptivity) where the Son receives being from the Father, to the commanding power directing the life of Jesus. The Son's identity as receptive in begottenness does not translate to a divine identity as receptive in the incarnation. Instead the Son's identity seems unmoored as the Son of the incarnation does not clearly reflect the identity of the Son generated in begottenness, which, according to these accounts, is where the Son's distinct personhood is grounded. The relationship between the Son of the incarnation and the Son of God's triune life becomes unclear. In a covenant ontology by contrast, the Son is eternally who the Son becomes in time as the God-human unity, Jesus. Thus, the receptivity of the Son extends both to the Son's identity within the immanent life of God and in God's economy of salvation, which isn't reflected in those Christologies that insist that the Son is the absolute agent and initiating power within Jesus.

To build his Christology Bruce McCormack draws from an unlikely ally in Cyril of Alexandria to develop a kenotic Christology that makes sense with the ontology he proposes. And it is this Christology that I believe gives even stronger foundation to Eiesland's disabled God. In my account the disability of God is not due to a violent act that renders God's body wounded such that the only way to affirm the "disabled God" is because of suffering and the crucifixion, which could be seen as reinscribing the link between impaired bodies and suffering and sin. Instead this ontology establishes God's mode of being as one who exists with ontological need, which provides further theological foundation to Eiesland's claim. Here the Son may be described as disabled, not strictly based upon the trauma he endured in time, but because he is revealed to be not independent eternally and to be specifically shaped for a relation of receptivity.

Kenotic Christology draws from the ancient Christic hymn preserved in the letter to the Philippians, which says that Jesus, though he was in the form of God, "emptied himself" (ekenosen) and "took the form of a servant," and "being found in human form humbled himself and became obedient even unto death."[6] Kenotic Christologies come in a variety of forms throughout history, and numerous studies detail the differing schools and approaches. What follows here is a simplified summary for the purpose of providing context for the approach to kenosis adopted in this book. In the following chapter I will address the critics of kenosis. Here, after a summary of the potential in kenotic Christology for a disability theology, I will address the problematic relationship between Barth's Christology and notions of obedience and submission.

Kenosis is typically associated with the self-emptying assumed to occur with the incarnation, when the Son took human form. Many theologians over the centuries associate this with the Son temporarily leaving behind certain properties considered natural to God for the sake of Jesus' earthly existence. Jesus says there are things he doesn't know but only the Father knows, because the Son has set aside omniscience or this property sits in repose, in willed non-use. Jesus says the one coming after him is more powerful than he, as he has set aside omnipotence.[7] Fierce debate raged among Reformed and Lutheran kenoticists around the extent of setting aside omnipresence, but generally speaking, because the pre-resurrected Jesus existed in the limits of a human body, the Son may be thought to have given up omnipresence as well. These properties are usually understood to be taken back up with the ascension, and thanks to the doctrine of the communication of properties, the divine property of omnipresence can be communicated to the human nature of Jesus, so that the real body and blood of Christ can be present on every altar around the globe at once.[8] Other theologians argued that it is the human nature that is more properly described as the one humbled and emptied; the human nature submits, does not presume equality with God as something to be grasped, and thus models for all humanity perfect humility before God and obedience to God.[9]

---

[6]Phil. 2:5-8.

[7]Associated with Gottfried Thomasius.

[8]This is associated with the Lutheran position. For a thorough account of the differing schools and developments through time, especially with emphasis on the Reformed and Lutheran debates, see Bruce L. McCormack, "Kenoticism in Modern Christology," in *The Oxford Handbook of Christology*, ed. Francesca Aran Murphy (Oxford: Oxford University Press, 2015). See also Coakley, *Powers and Submissions*, 3–39, and Anna Mercedes, *Power For: Feminism and Christ's Self-Giving* (New York City: T&T Clark, 2011).

[9]Associated with the Giessen school.

Yet there is another interpretation of kenosis dating at least to the fifth century with Cyril of Alexandria who understood kenosis not as the divestment of attributes proper to God but as the addition of a full human nature to the divine person. This addition is itself the abasement, or the self-humbling activity of the Logos. As previously noted, for Cyril the unity of the one subject was preserved by the divine overpowering the human, and his understanding of the *communicatio idiomatum* moved in one direction only: from the divine to the human.

Yet despite the weaknesses in Cyril's interpretation of kenosis, including this instrumentalization of Jesus' humanity, his explanation of kenosis as addition is promising for the Christology developed here. When paired with the covenant ontology described in Chapter 2, we can talk of a Logos shaped eternally for this addition of humanity, an addition that doesn't introduce change to God even as it makes humanity, or the creature, integral to the being of God eternally and essentially. Here kenosis does not refer to the Son setting aside majesty in order to enter into this state of receptivity, but the identity of the Son is shaped specifically for receptivity, to receive the full humanity of Jesus as God's own humanity.[10] And this is precisely how McCormack builds his constructive project by way of the eternal receptivity of the Son.

Christologies have traditionally preserved the divine–human unity of Jesus through the absolute activity of the Son over a passive and receptive human nature. Here instead, the Son receives from the human nature. McCormack explains, "The man Jesus acts and the Logos receives those acts as his own. The man Jesus experiences suffering and the Logos takes that suffering ... into his own being."[11] Unity is preserved through the performing agency of the human, received by the Logos as the real activity of the divine-human unity of Jesus. Thus "what Jesus experiences, God experiences,"[12] which offers further foundation to Eiesland's claim that God experiences disability because of Jesus' human experiences and the marks of that life retained in his ascension.

Explaining how this would then relate to those properties so often the topic of kenotic Christologies (omniscience, omnipotence,

---

[10]See McCormack, *The Humility of the Eternal Son.*
[11]McCormack, "Kenoticism in Modern Christology," 455.
[12]Bruce L. McCormack, "Divine Impassibility or Simply Divine Constancy?: Implications of Karl Barth's Later Christology for Debates over Impassibility." *Divine Impassibility and the Mystery of Human Suffering* 2009): 150–86 (p. 179).

etc.), McCormack says these weren't just set aside at the moment of incarnation (possibly to be reassumed at the resurrection), these were never assumed, as the Son is eternally in anticipation of precisely that incarnation where they are, in other kenotic frameworks, said to be set aside. "This means that the Son acts everywhere and always, in creation and redemption, in the power of the Spirit. The Spirit is the effective power of Father and Son."[13] The miracles performed by Jesus are through the power of the Holy Spirit, not directly by the Logos at work within Jesus. God qua Son does not deprive Godself of anything proper to God in willing "to act 'humanly' (in the power of the Spirit who indwells the man Jesus)."[14] And this suggests a need, a weakness even, in God as Son. The Son does not set aside power for incarnation; the Son is eternally constituted as one who relies upon the Spirit. As Barth states, "This helpless man was the almighty God. But the man who does not want to be helpless, who thinks that he can be his own helper, holds a view which is empty and futile and without substance."[15] Weakness, dependence, and receptivity are not outside the scope of what God can experience.

Further, while most discussions of the incarnation describe the Logos actively taking the human nature unto itself, McCormack stresses the ontological receptivity of the Logos such that the Logos does not actively assume the human nature, does not take it, but instead the Logos receives the humanity as a work of the Spirit.[16] McCormack describes his position in comparison to that of Puritan theologian John Owen who held

> the only active use of divine omnipotence on the part of the Word vis-à-vis His human nature lay in the assumption itself. All other works performed by Him were performed humanly, that is to say, in the power of the Spirit. ... I would not even make the assumption itself a direct work of the Son. I would say that all the Son's work is indirect, mediated by the Spirit who is at work in His human nature.[17]

---

[13]Bruce L. McCormack, "The Lord and Giver of Life: A Barthian Defense of the Filioque," in *Rethinking Trinitarian Theology: Disputed Questions and Contemporary Issues in Trinitarian Theology*, ed. Guilio Maspero and Robert Wozniak (New York: T&T Clark, 2012), 250.
[14]McCormack, "Kenoticism in Modern Christology," 456.
[15]*CD* IV/1, p. 459.
[16]McCormack, "The Lord and Giver of Life," 251.
[17]McCormack, "The Lord and Giver of Life," 251.

And so the fulfillment of God's triune life in the incarnation is not produced by the direct activity of the Logos, except indirectly as the Son breathes forth the Spirit together with the Father; the Son's identity is fulfilled in receiving the humanity through the Spirit.

In describing the Son's breathing forth of the Spirit with the Father, that is the eternal procession of the Spirit, McCormack describes it in terms of mission. "He breathes forth the Spirit to be the active agent who forms his human nature and unites Him to it."[18] The mission of the Son to be the God-human is assumed not only in the generation of the Son, but also by the mission and then procession of the Spirit for the fulfillment of this communion of God with humanity. "It must be remembered that this event of Self-constitution takes place with a definite goal and purpose in view, so that even in breathing forth the Spirit, the Son is already, by inclination and disposition, that which He will become."[19]

But what of the claims of the Gospel of John, affirmed in the creeds, that all things came into being through the Logos? This does not seem to cohere with an ontological state of receptivity. McCormack answers, "Jesus Christ is 'the motivating basis of creation'. He is not the 'effective agent' of creation in any sense other than that required by the Trinitarian axiom *opera trinitatis ad extra sunt indivisa*—the works of the Triune God directed beyond Himself to that which is other than Himself are indivisible."[20] The limitation of the Son assumed eternally in the generation of the Son for the purpose of incarnation is real, and not simply a linguistic affirmation or a temporary condescension of God.

McCormack explains that even Barth came close "to saying that it is the Holy Spirit who is most truly the effective agent in creating, rather than the Son. If Jesus Christ is the ground of the existence of creation, then the Spirit is its 'fundamental condition'."[21] This is not a denial of the scriptural witness to the role of the Logos, but qualifies that the Son's participation in creation is still through the Spirit. Because the work of the Spirit is clearly identified in Barth as that of "quickening and animation" of those coming to faith, it is "but a short step to say

---

[18]McCormack, "The Lord and Giver of Life," 252.
[19]McCormack, "The Lord and Giver of Life," 252.
[20]Bruce L. McCormack, "The Identity of the Son: Karl Barth's Exegesis of Hebrews 1.1–4 (And Similar Passages) in *Christology, Hermeneutics, and Hebrews: Profiles from the History of Interpretation*, ed. Jon C. Laansma and Daniel L. Treier (New York: T&T Clark, 2012), 170. Quoting Barth CD III/1 pp. 55–6.
[21]McCormack, "The Identity of the Son," 171, quoting CD III/1, p. 58.

that the Spirit is also the one who gave life to all things at the dawn of time."[22] If the ways of being within God, as Father, Son, and Spirit, are constituted for covenant, then "There can be no talk of the Spirit as the act of a communion between the Father and the Son which is not also, and at the same time, the act of turning towards the world in creative and redeeming power."[23] And here you see some hints of the folding of procession into the mission, that will be important to my argument developed here. The Spirit's constitution as creative and animating power for covenant is the same event as the Spirit's procession as the breath of the Father's call and empowerment of the Son's response, as the communion of love expressed in unified will for covenant.

Ontological Receptivity and Divine Vulnerability

Although McCormack pushes the ontological receptivity of the Son further than most, he does not assume this posture of receptivity to be as risky as other commentators do. For example, considering the chance that the Son's identity as eternally obedient may be thwarted if Jesus does not enact perfect obedience, McCormack comments: "But a God who has exhaustive foreknowledge will know what the man Jesus will do. Therefore, there is no 'dependence' in God on temporal events and if no 'dependence,' then no 'need' (in the customary sense of the word)."[24]

Others, however, find in Barth real risk in this venture. For example, Paul Dafydd Jones disagrees with those who claim God "fixed the outcome" of Jesus' life. According to Jones, Christ must "humanly achieve, enact and maintain obedience."[25] And, quoting Barth, he emphasizes that the history of the Son "plays itself out ... under the entire burden and in the entire danger of world history."[26] Although today we may see victory as assured, this does not alter the risk in

---

[22]McCormack, "The Identity of the Son," 171, quoting *CD* III/1, p. 57.
[23]Bruce L. McCormack, "The Lord and Giver of Life, 231.
[24]Bruce L. McCormack, "Processions and Missions: A Point of Convergence between Thomas Aquinas and Karl Barth," in *Thomas Aquinas and Karl Barth: An Unofficial Catholic-Protestant Dialogue*, ed. Bruce McCormack and Thomas Joseph White (Grand Rapids, MI: Eerdmans, 2013), 124.
[25]Jones, *The Humanity of Christ*, 225.
[26]*CD* IV/1: 215 rev.

the real history of Jesus' lifetime. "Christ had to effect this victory—and ... were he to have faltered, things would have turned out quite differently."[27] Jones asserts that there is "no assured path from cradle to cross,"[28] and movingly describes the risk of God's own heartbreak in this venture: "God took and takes the original risk of patience, the risk of having God's own heart permanently broken—shattered, even—when the Son assumes human flesh, and constitutes himself in terms of the life of Jesus Christ."[29] J. Kameron Carter makes a similar case for the risk of God in *Race: A Theological Account*, albeit without reference to Barth. He writes: "For when Mary gives birth to Christ, God not only becomes incarnate in a human being, but, more specifically, God's life is staked or dependent on woman. Dependent on Mary of Nazareth's fiat, the second Adam's human condition and potential to enact human redemption rests on the second Eve."[30] Which is to say: beyond God risking the fulfillment of God's identity in the human activity of Jesus, God also risks Godself to the will and care of Mary.

This is a promising feature of covenant ontology for disability theology: the introduction of vulnerability and need into the being of God. The Son relies upon the Spirit to empower the Son's own humanity. So too the Father risks, relying on the Spirit to guide Jesus in obedience toward the will of God, which ultimately is the fulfillment of the being of God, of the very purpose set forth in the self-constitution of God, which means that it is not only the identity of the Son that is risked. God hazards God's own being.[31] Or as Paul Dafydd Jones puts it: "God gives up thoroughgoing control over God's own being."[32]

On the one hand, this approach offers much to theologies with intentional concern for the oppressed and suffering: God enters into human life and experience at a reality and depth for which few other theological proposals have given foundation. However, the ontological receptivity of the Son may be read as reliant upon Barth's eternal obedience of the Son, which has a history that may

---

[27]Jones, *The Humanity of Christ*, 226.
[28]Jones, *The Humanity of Christ*, 226.
[29]Jones, *The Humanity of Christ*, 98.
[30]J. Kameron Carter, *Race: A Theological Account* (Oxford: Oxford University Press, 2008), 348.
[31]*CD* II/2, p. 161.
[32]Jones, *The Humanity of Christ*, 98.

be described as violent, and at minimum, harmful to many, especially women. As Barth's position considers a heterosexual marriage as a model reflective of the life of God, it lends support to long legacies of compulsory heterosexuality and the oppressions that entails. And so Barth's position has rightfully been attacked and rejected by scores of feminist theologians and theologians opposed to such a deification of heteropatriarchy. Thus, in what follows I confront this connection and propose a path forward that embraces vulnerability and receptivity in God's life but rejects Barth's analogy.

Eternal Subordination of the Son

Barth's close reading of the Trinity through revelation in Jesus, such that the eternal Son is understood to be Jesus Christ, led Barth to assert that the expression of Jesus' submission to the will of the Father not only demonstrates that the humanity of Jesus is obedient to the Father but reflects the eternal nature of the Son as well. For Barth the Father and Son subsist as a dynamic relationship in which One is obeyed and Another obeys.[33] The Son obeys the command of the Father in the economy because the Father and Son eternally subsist in a relationship established on begetting and being begotten. This relationship establishes their identities and is extended into the missions such that this posture of obedience is reflected in the Son's earthly life. Barth recognizes that this may create offense, but insists:

> We have not only not to deny but actually to affirm and understand as essential to the being of God the offensive fact that there is in God Himself an above and a below, a *prius* and a *posterius*, a superiority and a subordination. And our present concern is with what is apparently the most offensive fact of all, that there is a below, a *posterius*, a subordination, that it belongs to the inner life of God that there should take place within it obedience.[34]

Because the Son receives being from the initiative of the generation of the Father, this procession establishes an "above and below" based on the priority of order, "a prius and posterius," a before and an after (logical, not chronological). He claims that this eternal

---

[33]*CD* IV/1, p. 201.
[34]*CD* IV/1, pp. 200–1.

humility or obedience of the Son is not subordinationist, because this is said of one God, one subject in three ways of being. However, he also uses particular role assignments for men and women as a way to illustrate, by way of analogy, this internal relationship of God where one is determined to lead and one to follow, and so on. Thus, it is not surprising that many theologians reject this vision of God in the theologies of Barth and those influenced by it. Many charge that such an account deifies hierarchies, glorifying social structures and relationships whereby one has ultimate authority to whom another is obligated to submit and obey. Some contemporary evangelical theologians even explicitly link the eternal subordination of the Son to a divinely ordained subordination of woman to man, while insisting (as Barth did) that such submission does not mean lesser dignity.[35]

Though Barth goes to great lengths to reject the heresy of Subordinationism (which would claim Son and Spirit are ontologically inferior to the Father), his description of the triune life includes an explicit affirmation of "a superiority and a subordination," which surely implies to many readers an inferiority for the subordinate one below the "superiority" of the other.[36] Yet he denies this by stressing the unity of the one God who is both above and below within God's one existence. God is both the One who rules, leads, and commands, and simultaneously in God's second mode of being, the One who obeys, follows, and serves. He parenthetically suggests, however, in the midst of this discussion that we should reconsider the way we value these similar roles for husbands and wives in light of this divine arrangement.

Does subordination in God necessarily involve an inferiority, and therefore a deprivation, a lack? Why not rather a particular being in glory of the one equal Godhead, in whose inner order there is also, in fact, this dimension, the direction downwards, which has its own dignity? Why should not our way of finding a lesser dignity and significance in what takes the second and subordinate place (the wife to her husband) need to be

---

[35]See a range of perspectives covered in Dennis W. Jowers and H. Wayne House, eds., *The New Evangelical Subordinationism?: Perspectives on the Equality of God the Father and God the Son* (Eugene, OR: Pickwick, 2012).
[36]CD IV/1, p. 201.

corrected in the light of the *homoousia* of the modes of divine being?[37]

This comparison certainly does not help his case. Saying a wife has no less "dignity" than her husband in her subordination to him is offensive and upsetting to read, much less to embrace as divinely dictated, being grounded in the very being of God. And its use here and elsewhere undermines his insistence that this is not Subordinationist because we are speaking of One being in three modes and not of two or three distinct beings in a relationship. The same cannot be said for man and woman. And yet, as Lisa Stephenson argues, "For Barth, the order which is reflected in the interpersonal relation of male and female is initially an order found within the Trinity."[38]

Not wanting to shirk from a reckoning with Barth's troubling sexed and gendered language around this concept as it relates directly to the position I am building here, I will engage some of the literature relevant to my argument, before concluding with an account of receptivity and response as the Son's mode of being which I believe supports the concerns of disability theology without falling into the dangers of Barth's heteropatriarchal analogy of relation. I will seek to reconsider the terms we use to understand the identity of the Son, shifting from obedience and submission toward receptivity, though I understand an emphasis on receptivity is equally fraught with gendered and sexed stereotypes, and I will have to work hard to retain such a notion without reinforcing the gendered assumptions associated with it.

Analogy of Relation

Though these analogies of relation, drawing from heterosexual coupling to illustrate elements of the divine life, may figure more prominently in some of the theologies influenced by Barth's work on this, such as that of Hans Urs von Balthasar, we can trace some startling commonalities among them. In both Barth and

---

[37]*CD* IV/1, p. 202.
[38]Lisa P. Stephenson, "Directed, Ordered and Related: The Male and Female Interpersonal Relation in Karl Barth's *Church Dogmatics*," *Scottish Journal of Theology* 61 (4) (2008): 443–4.

Balthasar, for example, men and the Father are associated with action, agency, originality, leadership, and headship, and women are figured as passive, receptive, secondary, submissive, and subordinate. And as the Son derives being from the initiative of the Father, the Son is associated with the character of the woman in a heterosexual marriage. Barth configures a series of asymmetrical dyads with a structure of command–obey, lead–follow, and so on, from a relation of origin: be it logical (doctrine of processions) or chronological (his interpretation of the creation of humanity via Genesis 2). The Son receives his personhood from the Father, who is the origin of the divine life. Eve receives hers by God but from and after Adam.

In Barth's interpretation of Genesis 2 woman's identity as female is founded in her "being chosen," while the male identity is repeatedly associated with initiative and choosing.[39] Though Barth claims the relational structure he provides is not based on biology or reproduction (which would be a natural theology he rejects), he occasionally falls into physiological observations to justify his position nonetheless, for example:

> It cannot be contested that both physiologically and biblically a certain strength and corresponding precedence are a very general characteristic of man, and a weakness and corresponding subsequence of woman. ... [W]hat it means that man is the head of woman and not vice versa, is something which is better left unresolved in a general statement, and value-judgements must certainly be resisted.[40]

So here a physiological "strength" for man corresponds with "precedence," and "weakness" corresponds with women's "subsequence." Barth uses this unexamined assumption about physical ability to support his conclusions about the relevance of order in his analogy of relation: whose existence precedes and whose proceeds is determinative of one's role, or even one's identity. I will give some extended attention to the role of order in this structure for Barth, as order is foundational to the hierarchies associated with Barth's

---

[39]Faye Bodley-Dangelo, *Sexual Difference, Gender, and Agency in Karl Barth's Church Dogmatics* (London: T&T Clark, 2021), 144.
[40]*CD* III/2, p. 287.

theology, and I will argue that a covenant ontology upsets this order so that it can no longer serve to ground identity, be it God's or humanity's, or to support social hierarchies associated with gender, sex, or ability.

In a recent study on sexual difference in the theology of Karl Barth, Faye Bodley-Dangelo traces the connection between Barth's conception of male–female relation and parallel dyads throughout Barth's theology. Her work is primarily concerned with his theological anthropology, but because Barth insists he derives his theological anthropology from what humanity is revealed to be in Christ, his understanding of the incarnation and doctrine of God bear directly on his words about humanity and vice versa. What he interprets as fundamental humanity as male and female is reflected in how he illustrates various theological relationships: Father–Son, Yahweh–Israel, Christ–Church, the divine and human in Christ, and so on. Bodley-Dangelo demonstrates persuasively that Barth's assumptions about sexual difference are influenced by his social context but are uninterrogated despite how critical he is of other cultural and social elements at work within Germany of his day.[41]

Bodley-Dangelo identifies an "interpretive slide" in Barth's treatment of Adam and Eve that owes to Barth's precommitment to lifting Adam as a prefiguration of Christ and to Eve as a prefiguration of the Church. Thus, Adam and Eve, male and female, must be construed so as to fulfill particular roles that support his analogy of Christ to Church.[42] The Adam–Eve duality writ large is seen as foundational to God's creation and analogical to these other theological relations, including the relationship between God and humanity. In response to a question about analogies Barth said: "Husband and wife and their togetherness is such an image [of 'the covenant between God and man']. They are created together, and in their togetherness they reflect something of the relation between God and man. Man is not God. Certainly not! But in his

---

[41]Bodley-Dangelo traces the cultural associations within Germany around femininity and masculinity after the First World War—femininity blamed for Germany's defeat in the First World War and an elevation of masculine militarism during the rise of Nazism. The church also wanted to model itself on this image of masculine strength. Women became associated with maternity and preserving ethnic and spiritual purity (see Bodley-Dangelo, *Sexual Difference*, p. 131). Bodley-Dangelo explains, Barth "consistently avoids drawing from biological, reproductive, psychological, or sociological discourses for depicting the difference." And yet, "these unexamined assumptions, deeply embedded in social conventions, must do the heavy lifting" (196).

[42]Bodley-Dangelo, *Sexual Difference*, 148.

relation to woman, he reflects—Paul says it, not I—something of the glory of Christ and of God himself."[43] Barth repeatedly draws from this understanding of male/female relationships as "ranked, ordered, and determined" as an image for a variety of relations, with the "divine part" always ascribed to the male.[44] These descriptions of God and God's relationships, figured in this hierarchical binary and complementarian frame, quite obviously enforce a strictly heteronormative view of sexuality and companionship.

This ordering comes most famously (or perhaps infamously) to the fore in his discussion of man and woman in III/4 of the *Church Dogmatics*. There he writes:

> Man and woman are an A and a B, and cannot, therefore, be equated. In inner dignity and right A has not the slightest advantage over B nor does it suffer the slightest disadvantage .... A precedes B, and B follows A. Order means succession. It means preceding and following. It means super- and sub-ordination. It does indeed reveal their inequality. But it does not do so without immediately confirming their equality.[45]

Because Barth does not ground his understanding of humanity and the sexes in biology, his interpretation of Adam as prior to Eve and her derivative being from him as the original human carry the burden of his understanding of the identities that emerge in this relationship. And this is what founds the hierarchy he asserts with men as commanding leaders and women as obedient followers. Thus he creates the series of asymmetrical dyads based on order or sequence, comprising two types of actors: those who lead, command, and direct, and those who follow, obey, and respond; one is deemed active and the other, a passive recipient.[46]

In this frame, the divine is always associated with the masculine, except in the case of the Son within the inner life of God because the Son in that mode is receptive of life from the initiative of

---

[43]Karl Barth, "Theological Dialogue," *Theology Today* 19 (2) (July 1962): 171–7 (p. 173).

[44]Jason A. Springs, "Following at a Distance (Again): Gender, Equality, and Freedom in Karl Barth," *Modern Theology* 28 (3) (July 2012): 463.

[45]*CD* III/4, 169.

[46]According to Bodley-Dangelo this seriously distorts Barth's understanding of human agency (257).

the Father in generation; thus, the Son consents to the Father's sending, accepting the mission of the incarnation in obedience to the command of the Father. The Son's role is reversed however, in the incarnation itself. There the Son becomes the masculine principle to the femininized human nature that is submissive and obedient in Jesus.[47] Finally, the one subject of Jesus Christ (the God-human unity) remains the masculine bridegroom who leads the femininized Church, his bride, who follows. This relational structure within the life of God, even if only analogical, creates a defense for the perpetuation of a social hierarchy in which one can claim a sort of equality of worth and value while also consigning the sexes to roles that limit them to particular (heteronormative) relationships and functions within a strictly patriarchal frame. For example,

> in Barth's special ethics this ordering underlies his recommendation that women in abusive relationships should inspire men to better behavior through quiet self-restraint. This ordering manifests also in his depiction of the feminist movement as an envious grasping after the God-given agential prerogative of men. It is not surprising then that Barth has often been viewed as a poster-child for modern patriarchal theologies and, more recently, for heterosexist and complementarian theologies.[48]

Theologians have been grappling for decades with this power-differential read into human relationships based on the triune life of God by analogy. Some try to rescue Barth's analogy of relation through an emphasis on the perichoretic exchange among the Trinity as a way to upset the static hierarchy applied to the sexes, prioritizing Barth's trinitarian account of I/1 over his later reworking

---

[47]In the incarnation this slips so that the divine is the masculine agent to the obedient human nature. Elsewhere the analogy serves as illustration for the nature of Christ, Barth quotes 1 Cor. 11:3 "The head of the woman is the man" but pivots it to refer to the divine-human natures of Christ, such that Barth says Christ's "place" "is the place of man, [the divine nature] and his place of woman [the human nature]." He writes, "So little does this ascribe to man or refer to woman! So sharply and clearly is it determined and limited on both sides by what is primarily and properly the affair of Christ! His is the superordination and His the subordination!" *CD* III/2, 288. The differentiation of "One who is obeyed" and "Another who obeys" is also found in the two natures of the incarnation (*CD* IV/2, p. 208).

[48]Bodley-Dangelo, *Sexual Difference*, 11.

of the doctrine in light of election.[49] In contrast, Lisa Stephenson locates the problem as foundational to *CD* I, where Barth grounds the analogy of relation in origin and sequence, a "static relational order," later used to justify his reading of Adam and Eve.[50] She argues that the numerical labeling of the modes of being is indicative of the intractable nature of the ordering as foundational to the formal distinctions of God's eternal being: "there is a first, second, and third, because one follows after the other."[51] She explains: "Herein lies the problem. For the Trinity, the order present in the modes of being is an order of relations which is proper to God because the origin of relations, and the order which arises in this origin of relations, is constitutive of the distinct modes of being in the Trinity. The Father is Father because he is unbegotten, …" and so on.[52] On Stephenson's account the origin of relations as early as *CD* I lay the foundation for the asymmetrical dyads that only become more entrenched in subsequent volumes with Barth's reformulation of the doctrine of election as it "serves to further support the trinitarian basis for his ordering of the sexes when it all but collapses the economic Trinity into the immanent Trinity, embedding the ontological distinction between Creator and creature (and its order of origins) in the eternal electing will and communion of Father and Son."[53]

Upending Relations of Origin

I find this argument compelling: the scheme of super- and subordination is fixed to a conception of ordering for the divine life based upon the processions, then read likewise into humanity. The hierarchies are bound to these presumptions of ordering and sequence. Linn Tonstad has made a similar argument, taking issue with the very numbering of the divine persons and the emphasis throughout trinitarian theology on the determinative role of the processions.[54] She identifies the tendency toward analogies of sexual

---

[49]Alexander J. McKelway, "Perichoretic Possibilities in Barth's Doctrine of Male and Female," *Princeton Seminary Bulletin* 7 (3) (1986): 231–43.
[50]Stephenson, "Directed, Ordered and Related," 443.
[51]Stephenson, "Directed, Ordered and Related," 445.
[52]Stephenson, "Directed, Ordered and Related," 445.
[53]Bodley-Dangelo, *Sexual Difference*, 28.
[54]Linn Marie Tonstad makes a strong argument that sexual difference and hierarchy are bound up with an emphasis on processions and orders in the immanent Trinity. See

difference read into the divine life and the concomitant sexual hierarchy to be due at least in part to a theological dependence upon processions to make sense of distinction within God. Though Tonstad gives little attention to Barth, he is certainly guilty of a number of the moves of which she is so critical. She rejects the implicit subordinationism in many trinitarian theologies that figure the Son in eternal submission to the Father, rather than strictly the human nature in this posture of obedience. She describes theologians' attempts to claim that the submission of the Son is not a subordination as the ubiquitous "even though": "*even though* Jesus is subordinate or obedient to the Father in certain ways, *even though* the Son comes forth from the Father ... this is not true subordination."[55]

I agree with Tonstad and Stephenson that the priority given to the processions in constituting the identity of the triune God may be a primary culprit in the gendered and sexed framing of the Trinity and the implicit (or explicit) subordination of the "persons." And I agree that neither pointing to perichoresis, nor stressing the unity of divine action, will resolve the problem of the hierarchical structure rooted in Barth's Trinity that he extends to male–female relationships. Ascribing order as determinative of identity, role, and function is at the heart of the problem. The relationship of super- and subordination derive from the order of procession in Barth's theology, but I see a resource to counter this in the reframing of the Trinity in light of election. The chief critics of Barth's complementarianism identify the culprit of his sexual hierarchy to be his "dogmatic commitment to an all-powerful divine actor and subordinate, obedient human agent. They find that this commitment produces a recurring pattern of hierarchically ordered, dyadic relationships, wherein one actor leads and directs another."[56] It is the commitment to this arrangement that is read into the network of asymmetrical dyads throughout his corpus. However, here I am proposing the divine as recipient of the real spontaneous action of the human agent in Christ, which, together with the reconceptualization of the

---

"The Logic of Origin and the Paradoxes of Language: A Theological Experiment," *Modern Theology* 30 (3) (July 2014): 50–73. And her book *God and Difference: The Trinity, Sexuality, and the Transformation of Finitude* (New York: Routledge, 2016)
[55]Tonstad, *God and Difference*, 10.
[56]Bodley-Dangelo, *Sexual Difference*, 258.

relation of mission to procession, challenges this foundation for such hierarchical ordering.

Rather than strengthening the ordering of the sexes as Stephenson argues, a covenant ontology upsets the determinative nature of the ordering itself. Relations of origin are not constitutive of the trinitarian distinctions in covenant ontology, because it alters the relationship of procession to mission, granting priority to the missions, which determine the processions: the missions ground the processions as their ends. The Son's ontological receptivity is determined not strictly because of the Son's begottenness but because of the Son's intention for incarnation. The Son's identity as receptivity for humanity grounds the Son's begottenness, not vice versa. Order is no longer determinative of distinction and being, and thus can no longer provide a foundation for an ordering of sexed human life based on an order of creation. One might say, then, that any "ordering" that may be supposed in this ontology is for the sake of the humanization of God. Additionally, the role of the Son becomes shaped not by obedience to the Father first and foremost, but by receptivity for the inclusion of the humanity of Jesus.

Obviously, receptivity in and of itself will not unsettle the sexed and gendered connotations of the discourse, but I will challenge the heteropatriarchal and ableist assumption associated with receptivity. In the following chapter I will develop alternative metaphors for understanding theological relations that do not rely upon one's utter activity to the other's absolute passivity and surrender of agency, yet I will retain notions of receptivity and vulnerability.

Call–Response

The mission of the Son which establishes the Son's identity as one of receptivity, as I see it expressed here, is not a mission of submission or obedience as is often envisioned, but it is a mission of responding to a call, the taking up of a request, or assuming the task. If the threeness of God is grounded in mission for covenant, for relationship with God's creation, such that each "person" is constituted by and for that mission, there is less ground on which to assert the Father's role as commanding leader. Additionally, the Son relies on the Spirit to guide and empower, not on the Father, which may serve to elevate the Spirit to some prominence in the divine life uncommon in Western trinitarian frames. This shift then in identity for the Son from obedience to receptivity is significant, as one could also claim a shift in the identities of Father and Spirit. God desired covenant relationship and determined to shape God's eternal being for that purpose such that God the Father calls, the Son responds, and the Spirit enables the fulfillment of this will for covenant. It seems that "obedience" then is more properly attributed to the agency of the human nature of Jesus Christ who follows the guidance of the Holy Spirit.

This ontological receptivity of the Son (rather than ontological obedience) is not based on an order of processions to be analogically applied to human relations of order to presume a super- and subordination, or a command–obey dyad as we see in Barth and others. And in fact, the relation may be better conceived as a call–response. This results in the eternal call of the Father for relationship, simultaneous to the Son's response for incarnate life, that is the composite existence as the God–creature, which is also the receptivity of the Son.

Despite awkward attempts by some to argue that the name "Father" itself presumes a preeminence, an authority, the Son's reality simultaneously grants the Father's "identity," as the one who calls; the calling assumes the presence of the one who is called. We have a constitutive relationship established as call and response. We shouldn't assume a hierarchy because the one who calls is labeled Father. As anyone with aging parents knows, a parent can just as easily call out in need as a child would. I see this relationship of call and response as expressing a relationship of gift and reception. And the one who responds, receiving the call, is often the one who then offers the gift to the one who calls. Even the assumption, that is the Son's taking up of the call, is reliant on the Spirit who communicates the call, gives expression, and empowers the Son to accomplish it.

A call indicates a different nature of relationship to the one to whom it is directed than does "command." A call can be a request; a call can express a need; a call recognizes the freedom of the other. Couldn't the Father's call also be something closer to a supplication, a plea? A call from a place of need for the fulfillment of the life and will of God? And would this suggest the Father's own vulnerability in this venture on which God has staked God's own being? Speaking of the call of the Father also reinforces this shift in the posture of the Son from submission and obedience toward response. See, for example, Paul Dafydd Jones's description of this exchange in Christ: "In heeding and responding to the Father's call for loving fellowship with humankind ...."[57] and "Barth's suggestion is that the Son's economic action, the Son's incarnational 'becoming', *answers* the Father's eternal call for friendship with humanity. This answering of God's salvific intention is so radical that the Son freely takes on an identity that is bound to his incarnate existence."[58]

This exchange of call and response may be analogous to the lively interaction of preacher and congregation and signal a dependency upon each other to animate the ecstasy of the sermonic moment. Without the congregation's play that ecstasy is not breathed into the life of the communal experience. Typically this would be understood as a relationship in which the preacher calls and the congregation responds, but the congregation also calls to the preacher as response in the interchange. Kenyata Gilbert describes this as "trivocal preaching," including the preacher, congregation, and Holy Spirit, as the Spirit empowers the exchange so as to "enable the congregation to preach."[59] Longtime Dean of Howard Divinity School, Evans Crawford, describes this exchange in *The Hum: Call and Response in African American Preaching*, where he notes that even the beginning of the communal event of preaching may involve the invocation from the congregation in the form of an expression such as "Help 'em Lord!" This is not an authoritarian style of preaching as command and obey, but expresses a different communal exchange generated in relationship and mutual concurrence. He describes the relationship of call and response as not only a matter of talk-back, but also "feel-back," which includes gestures and body movement. The congregation's participation may be a groan, or a "hum." Crawford notes that some congregations participate in "preach-back," wherein those gathered understand that "while only one person had the title 'preacher,' in truth, it was the entire church that shared in the preaching."[60] The church together becomes "co-proclaimers."[61] Likewise, Harrison and Harrison describe the practice of call–response as an event that "seeks to synthesize

---

[57] Jones, *The Humanity of Christ*, 251.
[58] Jones, *The Humanity of Christ*, 207.
[59] Kenyatta R. Gilbert, "The Community's Sage: The Preacher's Call and the Congregation's Response," *Liturgy*, 35 (3) (2020): 17–24, 22.
[60] Evans E. Crawford, *The Hum: Call and Response in African American Preaching* (Nashville, TN: Abingdon Press, 1995), 56.
[61] Crawford, *The Hum*, 59.

'speaker' and 'listener' in a unified movement."[62] A passionate exchange occurs—while the preacher moves the congregation with the sermon, the congregation simultaneously moves the preacher "to a higher level of emotional feeling and understanding" of that Word.[63] When describing the call–response used by Martin Luther King Jr., Harrison and Harrison describe it as a "'calling *with*' those present, rather than a 'speaking *to*' an audience."[64]

This image of tri-dimensional call–response, empowered and enlivened by the work of the Spirit, is a better analogy for considering the missions that constitute the triune nature of God. It moves away from the reflex to hierarchical conceptions that derive from either orders of procession or relations understood as rooted in a command–obey dyad. Here we have the being of God as a Father who calls for relationship, a Son who answers, and a Spirit who enables the fulfillment of this desired communion in covenant. Here is a God who is vulnerable, who receives true human existence into God's eternal being, and who risks true human response to the guidance of the Spirit.

Conclusion

I challenge the notion common to many theologies that vulnerability, which could be understood here as need or dependence, must be denied to the being of God. Building from Cyril's understanding of kenosis as addition, but refusing his role reversal for the Son, positions the divine nature as receptive of human action. Here the man Jesus acts and the divine in Christ receives those acts as the Son's own. The man Jesus experiences suffering and the Son takes that suffering into the Son's own life. For the Logos to subsist in a state of receptivity, the Son needs something given, needs the

---

[62]Robert D. Harrison and Linda K. Harrison, "The Call from the Mountaintop: Call-Response and the Oratory of Martin Luther King, Jr." in *Martin Luther King, Jr. and the Sermonic Power of Public Discourse*, ed. Carolyn Calloway-Thomas and John Louis Lucaites (Tuscaloosa: University of Alabama Press, 1993), 162–78, 164–5. Quoting Jack Daniel and Geneva Smitherman, "How I Got Over: Communication Dynamics in the Black Community," *Quarterly Journal of Speech* 62 (1976): 33.
[63]Daniel and Smitherman, "How I Got Over," 36. Quoted by Harrison and Harrison, "The Call from the Mountaintop," 168.
[64]Harrison and Harrison, "The Call from the Mountaintop," 170.

other's offering. Receptivity is a relation; it assumes a gift given from another, and a gift taken up by the recipient. This should challenge the devaluation of vulnerability and receptivity, as it is God subsisting in such a posture, not the human nature. Surely this raises alarm bells for many orthodox theologians as it introduces an element of need in the divine life. If the human nature is the active agent, God may be vulnerable, dependent on the action of the human, putting God's will at risk.

To speak of the receptivity of the Logos in Christ is not to suggest a passive sublimation of the divine by the human nature. It is not simply to switch the divine–human roles in the same power binary where power and agency are held by one and denied the other. The power of the divine in Christ is neither unidirectional (top-down) nor unilateral. To posit the identity of the Son as receptivity is to understand the Son as relation: it is a posture of openness to the gift of the other, it assumes the one from whom one receives, it requires the other. This signals a productive power in intimacy, expressed in the willing reception of the nature and activity of the human of the union. And of course we must continue to remind ourselves when we speak of the ontological receptivity of the Son, we aren't positing an identity for the abstract *logos asarkos* sitting behind or before the Logos shaped particularly for the reception of humanity for the sake of loving communion with creation. The Son's identity as receptivity is always directed for this and should not be conceived in isolation from the union. And although we may consider the assumption of the humanity by the Son to be the Son's own work to bring about the union, it is more appropriate to recognize even this as the Son trusting the Spirit to bring about the communion that is the God-human unity of Jesus.

We mustn't assume that the receptivity is passivity. Jesus, the divine-human unity, is enlivened in the Son's active reception of the human. We are not forced into a dyad of active-passive in which the divine can only be utterly passive in Christ if the human nature is truly active and spontaneous. As McCormack explains, "There is no equivalence of the human as 'passive' (non-spontaneous) instrument of the Logos on Cyril's model and the 'receptive' Logos on mine. Indeed, 'ontological receptivity' is itself an active relation."[65] Here is a Christology that does not rely upon one's utter

---

[65]McCormack, *Humility of the Eternal Son*, 258.

activity to the other's absolute passivity and surrender of agency, to retain notions of receptivity and vulnerability. This should upset the rigid hierarchy at work in the analogy of relation described earlier that positions activity-receptivity as a binary opposition.

It may seem that I am suggesting the eternal receptivity of the Son is a desirable concept because those who are disabled are receiving care from non-disabled individuals, and thus it remains an image of nondisabled giver and disabled receiver, perpetuating a hierarchical image of charity and pity. But my point is otherwise. It is not the fact of receiving care, but rather the fact that everyone has gifts to give as well as needs to be met or responded to. I see this also in God as Father—the divine person who receives the identity as Father through the Son. Even so, by placing the receptivity on the divine side of the story in Jesus, it shifts the valuation away from the binary of giving care *versus* receiving care. If God is the receiver of gifts, and not only the giver of gifts, does that not begin to change the way we prioritize the two, such that we more easily recognize the agency of the receiver of care and value our interdependency as we see this within God's own identity as Son and in Christ? The doctrine of God won't support the masculinized patriarchal ideal when it is God who is vulnerable and humble. God embraces risk, not only because God momentarily experiences human vulnerability and humility during the thirty-three years of Jesus' earthly life, but because there is vulnerability within the being of God from eternity, as God stakes God's being on this venture. It is this revelation of the vulnerability within the life of God that turns patriarchal values on their head.

Debra Creamer writes of Eiesland's proposal: "The memorable image of the Disabled God, as one who intimately knows and even experiences disability, is especially important: in addition to calling for change, it irrevocably changes the way one encounters the Christian story. How can one be a Christian and not value experiences of disability? The image necessarily leads to changes in understanding and in action."[66] I believe this approach to the ontology of God gives significant doctrinal support to Eielsand's image of God.

---

[66]Debra Creamer, "Theological Accessibility: The Contribution of Disability," *Disability Studies Quarterly* 26 (4) (2006).

I admit to one significant reservation.[67] What does the claim that Jesus is identical with the second mode of God's being mean for already overly-masculinized depictions of the being of God? Do we now have a literal human male identified as an eternal hypostasis? How can this possibly help? Eiseland may offer us some assistance; she stresses, as do feminist theologians Ruether, Johnson, and others, that the significance here is on the real *flesh*, the physicality of the humanity taken into God's own life, not the (apparent) maleness of the physical body.[68] So we ought not choose a disembodied God out of fear of the concrete sexed embodiment of Jesus. It is more important to say that God has taken real human flesh as God's own, that God determined the very shape of God's existence for this inclusion of human life, the particular life and broken body of Jesus and all that reveals to us about God's solidarity with oppressed humanity. This fact of physicality is important to Eiesland and disability theologies. She explains: "deliberate attention to the physical body is necessary in order to prevent it from becoming socially erased or subsumed into notions of normal embodiment."[69]

In the next chapter I will further develop this notion of receptivity and how it may prove beneficial for a queer crip Christology. Understanding the identity of the Son as receptivity, instead of obedience or subordination, does not necessarily offer an escape from the history of women identified with this mode of being in complementarian theologies and in doctrines of God, but it does offer the potential to consider real vulnerability within the life of God, offering a revaluation of vulnerability and receptivity as a whole. Once receptivity is loosed from this sexed association, it offers promise and hope for many whose lives don't fit into the heteronormative framework that limits the imagination of so many trinitarian theologians.

---

[67]Of course, the intensely Christocentric nature of this proposal will not be acceptable to many postcolonial theologians and others who are pushing for advances in pluralist theologies and those accommodating to interfaith cross-pollination.

[68]Eisland, *The Disabled God*, 102. See also Reuther, *Sexism and Godtalk*, chapter 5, "Can a Male Savior Save Women?," 116–38; Elizabeth Johnson, *She Who Is: The Mystery of God in Feminist Discourse* (New York: Crossroads, 1992); and Sandra Schneiders, *Women and the Word: The Gender of God in the New Testament and the Spirituality of Women* (New York: Paulist Press, 1986).

[69]Eisland, *The Disabled God*, 22.

4

The Receptivity of God

Receptivity, Vulnerability, and Their Critics

As explained in the previous chapter, the case for the vulnerability of God established in the ontological receptivity of the Son is constructed through a kenotic Christology. Kenosis, however, has a troubled history with liberation theologies, especially feminist theologies. Feminists have debated kenotic Christologies for decades, perhaps most notably beginning with the exchange between Daphne Hampson and Sarah Coakley.[1] More recently, queer systematic theologian Linn Tonstad has joined the critics, targeting Sarah Coakley's retrieval of kenosis in particular. Those familiar with these debates may at first be surprised by a liberationist text embracing a form of kenoticism. Not only is kenoticism associated with a potentially dangerous expectation for people already oppressed to accept this situation as a righteous form of self-emptying, the interpretation proposed here further embraces receptivity as a divine mode of being, which may garner criticism for strengthening a binary in which the feminine is figured as passive receptivity bound to a masculine (penetrative) agency. This is certainly what Tonstad sees in theologies that share some similarities with the Christology proposed here. In what follows I will engage Tonstad's critiques in order to expose the need for the inclusion of disability theology in this conversation and to illuminate the ways this theological proposal upsets some of the

---

[1]Daphne Hampson, ed., *Swallowing a Fishbone? Feminist Theologians Debate Christology* (London: SPCK, 1996). For a full account, see Mercedes, *Power For.*

ableist and heteropatriarchal assumptions around female passivity and male agency taken for granted in some feminist rejections of kenoticism and vulnerability.

Tonstad details the sexed assumptions in trinitarian discourses that feature a masculine agency and feminine receptivity, which perhaps isn't named as explicitly in Barth as in her chief target, Hans Urs von Balthasar, but is nonetheless present in his analogy of relation. She uncovers how sexual difference is read into trinitarian theologies in ways that reinforce a compulsory heterosexuality, including the complementarity of the sexes used analogically for the divine life discussed previously. She also identifies compulsory heterosexuality in theologies that in various ways expect one to make room for the other. The result, according to Tonstad, is a structure requiring penetration and a receptive womb-wound: one active agent to the self-sacrifice of the emptied recipient. The sexed analogy of relation is a heterosexual one, figured primarily by procreative heterosexual coitus, harkening back to the womb as a presumed recipient of the life-infusing agency of the phallus. Once this subtext is exposed, it is hard to deny its underlying influence across theological traditions.[2]

One theologian Tonstad takes to task on this matter is Graham Ward, who, though seeking to develop a theology that is inclusive of diverse bodies and sexualities, fails to move outside the heterologics bound up with the womb-wound. Ward, like Eiesland, sees the wounds of Christ in his resurrected body as a site rife with theological possibilities. He focuses particularly on the side wound as evidence of a resurrected intersex Christ: Thomas's probing finger, imaged by Caravaggio in *The Incredulity of Thomas*, suggests a vaginal opening for Thomas's penetration.[3] Further, the side wound becomes a womb in depictions of Christ birthing the church. Here Ward interprets the rush of water and blood from the gash in Jesus' side (Jn 19:34) as symbolic within John's gospel "of the vaginal opening through which the community of Christ's body is born."[4] Thus, Ward describes a resurrected Jesus who is both male

---

[2]Tonstad, *God and Difference*.

[3]According to Ward, following the resurrection, Jesus' body bears "the marks in his flesh of both the male and female sex—without his being androgynous." Graham Ward, *Christ and Culture* (London: Blackwell Publishing, 2005), 150. He thus asserts that Jesus is resurrected "as a hermaphrodite." Graham Ward, "There Is No Sexual Difference," in *Queer Theology: Rethinking the Western Body* (Oxford: Blackwell Publishing, 2007), 78.

[4]Ward, "There Is No Sexual Difference," 78.

and female based upon the presumed visibly discernable male and female genitalia on his resurrected body.

Tonstad, though appreciative of Ward's intention to construct a theology inclusive of queer bodies, is highly critical of his adoption of the womb-wound. Following Irigaray, Tonstad rejects images of the side-wound as womb as beneficial for women. Christ feminized through his wounding and suffering perpetuates heteropatriarchal patterns of abuse and reinscribes the ubiquitous symbolics of female penetrable receptivity and male phallic agency. Further, the feminization of Jesus' body through his crucifixion strengthens the linkage of female embodiment to death, which is deleterious to women's actual bodies and lives. She associates the receptivity of the body of Christ here with a binary that is deeply misogynist and heterosexist.

She also challenges the notion found in various theologies that such suffering (the womb-wound) is eternalized in the being of the Son, which is likely true of the theology I develop here with my claim that the impaired body of Christ is anticipated eternally and proleptically identified with the humanity of the Son. Tonstad rejects any suggestion that suffering and death belong to the being of God, and she upholds God's impassibility, conceding only that in Christ God suffers impassively.[5] Let me be clear, however, the eternal impairment of the Son that I affirm with Nancy Eiesland does not equal eternal suffering. Is the broken body of Christ the result of horrific suffering? Certainly. But to assert that the eternally impaired body means an eternally suffering body is to reinscribe cultural assumptions that impairment necessarily means a life identified with lack and pain. The assertion of the eternally impaired body of Christ is a claim for the full humanity of God the Son from the founding and self-constituting decision of God to be for and with humanity. It is an affirmation that the disabled body truly is *imago dei*, and even more. An even stronger support for Eiesland's disabled God comes from the eternal receptivity of the Son, as it resists the assumption that need is inherently a debasement or a quality necessarily lesser than to be without need. The receptivity of the Son signals the eternal value of interdependence and life intertwined in care, reception of care, and assistance in care.

---

[5]Tonstad, *God and Difference*, 11.

Tonstad takes issue with theologies that make virtuous one's retraction of oneself for the sake of the other. Such forms of self-emptying are often associated with kenotic Christologies, but can also be found in accounts of creation where God must retract Godself in order to make a space for God's creation to exist.[6] She identifies similar moves in some ecclesiologies and eschatologies, and we can see an example in Ward's description of the ascension: "The withdrawal of the body of Jesus must be understood in terms of the Logos creating a space within himself, a womb, within which (*en Christoi*) the church will expand and creation be recreated."[7] Following this pattern, model relationships require one to retract to make room for the other, or for one to have room within oneself for the penetrating presence of the other. Tonstad writes,

> I use the term "womb-wound" to indicate images of relationships that assume good relation between persons (divine or human) require making room for another (the spatialization of the womb often associated with rendering "woman" into a place for the becoming of the other) through sacrificial forms of (something like) suffering. Womb-wound imagery is … fundamentally heterosexual, and it sets up another "incarnation" of sexuality and sexual difference in God.[8]

In contrast to Ward, for Tonstad, Jesus' resurrected body reveals abundance of room to come alongside one another in close and intimate contact, without a submissive recipient of the other's imposing presence. Tonstad is surely inspired by what Judith Butler calls Irigaray's "rigorous anti-penetrative eros of surfaces,"[9] which leads to Tonstad's suggestion that the clitoris is a more fitting metaphor for relations as it signals surface touch, and stands outside of the phallic-penetrative frame of reproductive heterologics. Tonstad explains, "Clitoral pleasure becomes a sign of resurrection …. The uselessness of the clitoris in reproduction … signals … the possibility

---

[6]She doesn't address Moltmann directly on this but his interpretation of "zimzum" seems an obvious target.

[7]Graham Ward, "Bodies: The Displaced Body of Jesus Christ," in *Radical Orthodoxy: A New Theology*, ed. John Milbank, Catherine Pickstock, and Graham Ward (London: Routledge, 1999), 176.

[8]Tonstad, *God and Difference*, 13.

[9]Judith Butler, *Bodies That Matter: On the Discursive Limits of Sex* (London: Routledge, 1993), 19.

of nonreproductive sexuality beyond the pleasures of submission, penetration, and (self-) shattering."[10] The doctrine of God and Christology developed here, with an eternally impaired Son identified with receptivity seems primed for Tonstad's critique. However, as I will argue here, I believe much is lost when we refuse notions of receptivity or interdependence in the divine life and in God's life with us.

Kenosis in Feminist Theology

Tonstad is not alone in her feminist concern with the concept of kenosis. Though Rosemary Radford Ruether famously uses the term in *Sexism and Godtalk* to speak of the kenosis of patriarchy in the life of Jesus,[11] it has a troubled history within feminist theology because the Philippians hymn charges the reader to have this same attitude as was in Christ who emptied himself, took the form of a slave, and was obedient unto death. Feminist theologians note that far too often women alone are expected to take this role while men are directed to headship, and you can see why, when the human nature in Christ and his submission to the divine is explicitly feminized throughout the vast corpus of theological literature even to the present. In this context, the charge to submit is rightly suspect.

Inherent in this critique, however, is a stance common among early white feminists that rejects notions of vulnerability, dependency, and surrender altogether as dangerous for women. Such positions within feminism quickly drew critique from disabled theorists who note that movements of female empowerment have often adopted language and values from modern liberalism, such that the agenda of activism has centered independence and autonomy in a way that further marginalizes women with disabilities.[12] Feminists too often argue for women's liberation in ways that denigrate the lives of women deemed physically weak or in need of assistance. Susan Wendell charges that "Until feminists criticize our own body ideals

---

[10]Tonstad, *God and Difference*, 275–6.

[11]Ruether, *Sexism and God-Talk*. Jesus gives up patriarchal privilege, or empties himself of powers associated with the patriarchy.

[12]Rosemarie Garland-Thompson says this is "One of the most pervasive feminist assumptions that undermines some disabled women's struggle." In "Re-shaping, Re-thinking, Re-defining: Feminist Disability Studies" (Washington, DC: Center for Women Policy Studies, 2001), https://www.ces.uc.pt/projectos/intimidade/media/Re-shaping%20re-thinking%20re-defining.pdf (accessed October 18, 2022).

and confront the weak, suffering, and uncontrollable body in our theorizing and practice, women with disabilities and illness are likely to feel that we are embarrassments to feminism."[13] Doreen Freeman brings this critique to feminist theology, arguing that disabled women "embody all that the blossoming feminist does not want to be," as disabled women often "reinforce the stereotypes as 'passive, dependent, needy' recipients of care."[14] She asks if feminists can celebrate the body as an image of the divine if it is a "deformed, leaky, sometimes smelly, constantly fatigued, psychotic, [and/or] dysfunctional body." She charges that in its emphasis on "wholeness of mind, body and spirit," feminist theology leaves the disabled woman "negated, isolated and alienated."[15] From a different perspective queer theologian Marcella Althaus-Reid states the greatest fear in theology may well be "the horror of uncontrolled bodies."[16] She is here referring to the bodies of those whose sexuality is deemed out of control, but disability theologians also note the church's deep fear of bodies that are not controlled, whose movements shake, seize, and palsy, and whose voices shout, grunt, or click, bodies that do not sit still and keep silent in pews, bodies that may spill the consecrated wine with a tremor, bodies that upset their tidy theodicies. Sadly, feminist theologies have erred in these ways as well. Many have challenged the way theology has written "proper" masculinity and femininity into understandings of God and Christ that serve to perpetuate oppressive structures. But disability theorists remind us that sick and impaired bodies are often doubly marginalized by even these liberationist discourses. When feminists reject vulnerability who else is impacted? When feminists view receptivity as a uniquely feminine mode of being, which is oppressive, and thus to be repudiated, who else is harmed?

Many disability theologians have exposed the need for theologies to reckon with vulnerability in honest and affirming ways. Coakley also questions the sweeping rejection of vulnerability in her treatment of kenotic Christology. She writes, "there is another, and longer-term, danger to Christian feminism in the *repression* of all forms

---

[13]Susan Wendell, *The Rejected Body: Feminist Philosophical Reflections on Disability* (New York: Routledge, 1996), 93.

[14]Doreen Freeman, "A Feminist Theology of Disability," *Feminist Theology* 10.29 (2002), 77.

[15]Freeman, "A Feminist Theology of Disability," 77.

[16]Marcella Althaus-Reid, *The Queer God* (New York: Routledge, 2003), 47.

of 'vulnerability,' and in a concomitant failure to confront issues of fragility, suffering, or 'self-emptying' except in terms of victimology."[17] She asks why "'vulnerability' *need* be seen as a 'female' weakness rather than a (special sort) of 'human' strength."[18] Coakley follows the tradition that interprets kenosis as the human nature's surrender to the divine, and follows Ruether to a point, as it is the male Jesus, who in surrender and humility, empties patriarchal values: here Jesus chooses "*never to have* 'worldly' forms of power," and thus eschews a power we assume he could have possessed.[19] Yet further, for Coakley kenosis points specifically to the surrender of the "vulnerable" human nature to the power of God, and she calls Christians (regardless of sex) to surrender to God in our spiritual path to union with God. "Self-emptying" here is not self-abasement, nor a negation of self, but "the place of the self's transformation and expansion into God."[20]

Coakley follows a tradition that identifies the surrender, submission, and humility of Jesus as precisely a revelation of perfect humanity, and will not entertain the idea that it is the divine revealed to be vulnerable in Jesus. She frames her treatment of kenosis with the experience of contemplative prayer, calling it a "vulnerable activity of 'space-making,'" and describing the practice as the "*special* 'self-effacement' of this gentle space-making—this yielding to divine power which is no worldly power."[21] The reader can anticipate Tonstad's critique here as Coakley frames kenosis as the call for humanity to "make space" within ourselves for the indwelling of God.

Though Coakley pushes against a kenoticism that would have the divine utterly control the human nature, which would fuel "masculinist purposes, masculinist visions of the subduing of the weaker by the stronger,"[22] she explicitly rejects theologies that portray the "human limitations of Jesus" as a "positive expression of his divinity rather than a curtailment of it."[23] The vulnerability revealed in Jesus can only be a "curtailment" of the divine and cannot be figured as the revelation of the divine nature in Christ. She opposes kenotic

---

[17]Coakley, *Powers and Submissions*, 33.
[18]Coakley, *Powers and Submissions*, 33.
[19]Coakley, *Powers and Submissions*, 31.
[20]Coakley, *Powers and Submissions*, 36
[21]Coakley, *Powers and Submissions*, 35.
[22]Coakley, *Powers and Submissions*, 15–16.
[23]Coakley, *Powers and Submissions*, 23.

Christologies that would identify God as "permanently 'limited'"
because of the incarnation, and she asks: "Does this not then also
make God intrinsically non-omnipotent and non-omniscient (as
opposed to temporally non-omnipotent and non-omniscient under
the conditions of the incarnation)?"[24] She argues that this approach,
which surely includes Eiesland's disabled God, "shear[s] God down
to human size," and makes "God intrinsically power*less*, incapable
of sustaining the creation in being."[25] Anna Mercedes sums up
well the failure in Coakley's proposal: "Rather than undoing
gender stereotypes through her Christology, she instead lumps all
humanity, in Christ, into a feminized state of submission beneath a
traditionally masculinized deity, thus reinstating the dichotomy of
a masculine power and female submission, and between masculine
divinity and feminine materiality."[26]

Even though Coakley's kenosis does not result in a humility
within God qua Son, which Tonstad also rejects, the human emptied
for God's indwelling smacks of too much penetration and womb-
wound for Tonstad.[27] Though she agrees that the obedience we
witness in the life of Jesus to the will of the Father in the gospels
belongs to the human nature and not the Logos, Tonstad argues
that obedience and humility are overcome eschatologically, and are
not an ultimate model for human relation, even to God. Tonstad
argues that Coakley's account of the hypostatic union, reliant on
a human self-emptying obedience, which becomes a metaphor for
"human sexual union," works within the passive-active binary.
Tonstad writes, "Of course this metaphor is one of heterosexual
union, even if no merely passive femininity is assumed, and the
kenotic relationality that undergirds this series of metaphors is one
in which a divine bridegroom, without lack or self-emptying, pours

---

[24]Coakley, *Powers and Submissions*, 23
[25]Coakley, *Powers and Submissions*, 24.
[26]Mercedes, *Power For*, 35.
[27]Interestingly, later in her book Tonstad affirms a kenosis of addition, still read as
the obedience and humility of the human—and all for its eschatological overcoming.
She speaks of the "'additive' nature of the incarnation" (*God and Difference*, 232),
and says "Kenosis does not mean loss and self-emptying; it means that the Lord of
Glory takes on humanity in all its abasement. Obedience and humility are means,
not ends, and they are means oriented toward their own overcoming" (*God and
Difference*, 233–4). There is no real vulnerability and it has no eschatological value;
it is disallowed from God's being.

his fullness into the actively desirous receptacle of his human bride (Christ's human nature)."[28] She identifies in Coakley's contemplative case for kenosis, the human as an "active passive," for whom "feminine or human activity is active self-emptying of one's noetic faculties, an active passivity of waiting on God by willfully choosing to make space for the God whose emission fills one."[29]

My disagreement with Coakley is on different grounds. Though I agree with her that the standard, uncritical, impulse to reject all vulnerability is flawed, especially from the perspective of disability, I disagree with Coakley's refusal of any element of vulnerability within the life of God. It is this revelation of vulnerability within God that turns these patriarchal values on their heads. God's acceptance of vulnerability in the triune life, by hazarding God's own being on this mission to covenant, and taking true human existence and experience as constitutive of God in God's second way of being, ultimately shatters the assumptions of autonomy, independence, and power as force as supreme values.

My concern is that by forestalling all suggestion that there is within God a need, or a critical dependency, we retreat to a God that is only sheer power, independence, and autonomy. Yes, we must denounce the gendered stereotypes and heteronormativity behind much systematic theology, but we should not do so in a way that simultaneously denigrates the lives of those whose dependency and need are most visible. Do we flatly reject covenant ontology because some will wrongly identify receptivity with an assigned role for women? Or do we allow the vulnerability of God to transvaluate our appraisals of human life?

My proposal reimagines what desired power looks like as the vulnerability within Christ demonstrates God's own risk not only in the incarnation but also in God's self-constitution as triune. By highlighting the relationality of the power in encounters within the disability and queer communities, this model rejects the heteronormative assumption that such relationships rely on one's domination of another whose agency is lacking or quashed. I hope finally by understanding receptivity as a significant vulnerability within the Logos, and thus the divine life, that I will amplify Eiesland's efforts to revalue the vulnerability and the need of human

---

[28]Tonstad, *God and Difference*, 104.
[29]Tonstad, *God and Difference*, 105.

lives, by showing these dispositions thriving within the eternal essence of the triune God.

Queer Crip Christology

In heteronormative Christologies the human nature (figured as feminine despite Jesus' male body) was assumed to be passive to the dominating divine nature in Christ (figured as masculine power). But in the ontological receptivity of the Son, this assumption of the divine masculine dominant (penetrator) paired with the submissive (receptive) human is overturned. This understanding of the hypostatic union upsets these assumptions of receptivity as feminine-submissive and belonging to the realm of the human (or lesser) nature, and it forges a different expression and understanding of power. Here the divine offers Godself as receptive, not surrendering divine agency, but neither obliterating human agency and spontaneity (real decision and action). This figuring of the union pushes our imagination outside the heteropatriarchal dictates of intimacy and configurations of power bound to dyads of command–obey that strip agency and will. As Eiesland says, "The disabled God does not engage in a battle for dominance or create a new normative power, God is in the present social-symbolic order at the margins with people with disabilities and instigates transformation from the de-centered position."[30] The power from the bottom, from the margins of the margins, manifests differently from that emerging in the dominant centers. These moves serve to resist the heteronormative patriarchal marking of receptivity as inherently passive and feminine, and give a theological foundation for the revaluation of dependency.

Tonstad's critique of the heteropatriarchal legacy in systematic theology is stunning, and her offer of the clitoris as an alternative signifier of proper relations certainly pushes the imagination away from the "stranglehold" of heteropatriarchal thinking,[31] but its rejection of receptivity (seemingly because receptivity requires a concomitant penetration) has other consequences and leaves her

---

[30]Eiesland, *Disabled God*, 100.
[31]See José Esteban Muñoz, who talks about the "stranglehold" of straightness and straight time. *Cruising Utopia: The Then and There of Queer Futurity* (New York: New York University Press, 2009), 32.

vulnerable to the critique Butler levies against Irigaray as Tonstad "forecloses the possibility of female-to-female [and male-to-male, as well as female-to-male] penetrative and interpenetrative eroticism."[32] Though she is right to denounce the dominant misogynist and heterosexual analogical associations in systematic theology, she appears to accept penetration as always figured as male and penetrability as female, staying within a heterosexual matrix that never shakes the stability of the assumed and assigned sexed positions. By reading all movements of penetration-receptivity as inherently reflective of hetero-procreative sex, Tonstad unintentionally reinscribes it, and unfortunately concurs with images of the masculine as the virile agent. Thus she retains the phallocentric reading of agency, even as she seeks to push the Christian imagination away from this fixation.

In an interesting turn in Tonstad's argument, she accepts some form of receptivity in the divine life, commonly associated with perichoresis, each "person" gives to and receives from the others. However, as she seeks an alternative location for distinct "personhood" beyond origin, she claims that it is the particular giving of each that determines their identity. She sees the relations that are constitutive of persons to be "gift-circulation."[33] The act of giving becomes the determinative act for each personal distinction. "All give, but in different ways, and those different ways *are* their divine personhood."[34] The "persons" share in the receptivity of the gifts, but they each receive differently based

---

[32]Amy Hollywood, "That Glorious Slit: Irigaray and the Medieval Devotion to Christ's Side Wound," in *Luce Irigaray and Premodern* Culture, ed. Elizabeth Harvey and Theresa Krier (London: Routledge, 2004), 120. See Butler, *Bodies That Matter*, 50–1.

[33]Tonstad writes,

> Doing away with the concept of generation allows for something like the exchange of gifts between the Spirit and Son on Tanner's account to expand to include the entire trinity, including the Father. Each person gifts something to the others, or better, the persons give the same thing in different modes (for in God there is no-*thing* to give, since the persons are God by nature and identical with the divine essence). These asymmetrical exchanges are triadic intransitive relations. The persons (as persons) are nothing aside from their relations to each other. These relations are circular and reversible in that each person is both a giver and a receiver, but they are irreversible in the mode of giving and receiving in each case. (*God and Difference*, 229)

[34]Tonstad, *God and Difference*, 229.

on the shape of their personhood, which is determined by the gift they give.[35] Giving can shape the divine life, but receptivity cannot, because receptivity is suggestive of a womb, of a space for receiving from another, and Tonstad's proposal will not accept this for persons, divine or human. And here again she falls back to associating receptivity with passivity even as she says the words active and passive would be better not used: "the persons are always 'active' and 'passive' (although it would be better to avoid that terminology altogether); in relation to each other as to us, they are all always working together in different ways, giving and receiving at the same time."[36] I wonder how much masculinist assumption lies behind this claim that in God only giving can be determinative of divine personhood and receiving remains linked with passivity. While she is highly critical of Coakley's commitment to human vulnerability before God, she shares a similar commitment to a God of power, rejecting any notion of the vulnerability of God.

Her metaphor of clitoral touch may be a useful corrective, but I believe the association of receptivity with strictly heterosexual relationships is shortsighted and less fruitful for disability theology, as interdependency and the exchange of need and gift is a rich resource for affirmative theologies of body and difference. I fear that by surrendering receptivity (and thus vulnerability) to the dominant religio-cultural symbolics, we lose the opportunity to radically reconceive their nature and value. Additionally her rejection of receptivity as an eschatological value disallows a future of interdependence, of interpenetrability and receptivity of giving and receiving in resurrected life, which not only has potential implications for the appraisal of sexuality but also other forms of embodiment and care. I resist the conclusion that any posture of receptivity in our conception of the divine life means a heterosexual framing of this relationship and association with the womb. Similarly her suggestion that the Son's receptivity inherently suggests a subordinated position is sustained only

---

[35]"Since each person gives differently, the reception (but not the gift) in each case is sharable: the Father and Spirit both receive from the Son, but differently. Since all three do the same thing in different ways, the particularity of the recipient shapes the gift as well. The relations are therefore noninterchangeable and irreducible" (Tonstad, *God and Difference*, 229).
[36]Tonstad, *God and Difference*, 229.

if receptivity is read through the lens of heteropatriarchal preconceptions of that position and is figured as passive. However, as I argued previously when mission drives procession, trinitarian "personhood" is bound not to order, but to covenant, thus upsetting the inherent hierarchy she identifies with the ordering, and because the ordering doesn't determine identity, the implicit subordination is unfounded.

In the previous chapter I highlighted ways in which trinitarian relations are read back into human relations and vice versa. The analogy that is to give us insight into the triune life is one of sexual complementarity: the male figured as active initiator and the female as passive recipient. This has obvious sexual connotations as well, mirroring heterosexual intercourse. I certainly agree that the analogy of relation that gives life to the doctrines of Trinity and hypostatic union is gendered, sexed, and sexual. The doctrine of God and Christology shouldn't buttress heterosexuality any more than it should enforce the subjection of women. Nor should our theologies support ableism. People with disabilities are typically marginalized by the same forces of heteropatriarchy. Where society and religion inscribe strict norms of behavior and performance of gender and sex, those with different or nontypical embodiments are oppressed. And so these sexed, gendered, and sexual assumptions behind our doctrines of God and Christ will directly impact the acceptance of bodies with disabilities. Heteronormativity is bound up with heteroableism, and people with disabilities often understand their sexuality to be figured as "queer" either by society or embraced as their sexual identity.

I agree with Tonstad that we shouldn't suppose that just because one can now identify a womb in the body of Jesus for the birthing of the church that this is necessarily a beneficial site for women to identify with Christ. But I further contend we should not assume receptivity to be womb-like. I've argued elsewhere that an overemphasis on womb and motherhood in feminist theology is alienating to many women without wombs or who do not give birth.[37] Further, normative sex read into the very structure of the Godhead marginalizes more than women and those who identify

---

[37]See Lisa D. Powell, "The Infertile Womb of God: Ableism in Feminist Doctrine of God," *CrossCurrents* 65 (1) (March 2015): 116–38.

as queer; it also further marginalizes the sexuality of many in the disability community. I will press the analogy here, looking for other relationships to loose this binding of the Trinity to heteropatriarchal marriage. If we are going to accept the deep worth of receptivity/ vulnerability, then we must challenge these associations with alternative images. If we are going to consider what the Son as receptivity may mean for sex, gender, and sexuality, we must also pay attention to how these intersect with disability. We will find that receptivity can exist as an active modality.

Queer Crip Sex

Perhaps breaking free entirely of sexual imagery and metaphor would be useful, however receptivity has a long history of theological and cultural associations that cannot simply be overcome by ignoring them. Consider the history of theological musings on women as receptacles for male seed (understood as life) from the Hebrew scriptures onward.[38] And we see this cultural association of procreation with women as passive recipients of male phallic initiative even in medical texts as has been demonstrated by Emily Martin in her much-anthologized essay "The Egg and the Sperm: How Science Has Constructed a Romance Based on Stereotypical Male-Female Roles."[39] False cultural associations of women with passive receptivity and men with active initiation has impacted medical accounts of conception, and innumerable other cultural and religious discourses. These ideas must be challenged head on.

Marcella Althaus-Reid argued that "theology is a sexual act," "a sexual ideology performed in a sacralizing pattern."[40] And because Tonstad is right that these sexed analogies pervade theological discourse in ways that ground and maintain sexism, heteronormativity, and I would add ableism, the best way forward is not to avoid sexual analogy altogether, thus ceding that territory

---

[38]See Laura Quick, "Bitenosh's Orgasm, Galen's Two Seeds and Conception Theory in the Hebrew Bible," *Dead Sea Discoveries* 28 (2021): 38–63.

[39]Emily Martin, "The Egg and the Sperm: How Science Has Constructed a Romance Based on Stereotypical Male-Female Roles," *Signs* 16 (3) (1991): 485–501.

[40]Marcella Althaus-Reid, *Indecent Theology: Theological Perversion in Sex, Gender, and Politics* (London: Routledge, 2000), 87.

to the heteropatriarchal ableist imagination, but to complicate these sexed associations through alternative readings and metaphors in ways that reconstruct doctrines in the lineage of tradition but in ways that enhance the full flourishing of the lives and faith of people with disabilities.

Crip theorists have convincingly argued that queer and disabled bodies are marginalized through a similar web of oppressive normativity. Robert McRuer explains that "compulsory ablebodiedness" is "thoroughly interwoven with the system of compulsory heterosexuality."[41] Likewise Alison Kafer charges that "what is needed, then, are critical attempts to trace the ways in which compulsory able-bodiedness/able-mindedness and compulsory heterosexuality intertwine in the service of normativity; ...to speculate how norms of gendered behavior—proper masculinity and femininity—are based on nondisabled bodies; and to map potential points of connection among, and departure between, queer (and) disability activists."[42] Tonstad has done such tracing of heteronormativity and heterosexism, and numerous studies in disability theology have likewise traced the normative use of nondisabled bodies and ableism in scripture interpretation, theological anthropology, ecclesiology, and pastoral care. Here I further the work by drawing the concerns of crip sexuality into the theological conversation.

Tobin Siebers, McRuer, Kafer, and others describe ways in which disabled people constitute a significant sexual minority as "the sexual activities of disabled people do not necessarily follow normative assumptions about what a sex life is."[43] Siebers considers crowded housing situations and health-care facilities where residents do not have privacy or ways to mitigate when and who enters their rooms. He asks the reader to imagine "Do Not Disturb" signs on doors in medical or care facilities.[44] People in care in such institutions are not offered privacy, are not granted rights to limit access to their

---

[41]Robert McRuer, *Crip Theory: Cultural Signs of Queerness and Disability* (New York: New York University Press, 2006), 2.

[42]Alison Kafer, *Feminist, Queer*, 17. She further calls on the discipline "to examine how terms such as 'defective,' 'deviant,' and 'sick' have been sued to justify discrimination against people whose bodies, minds, desires, and practices differ from the unmarked norm" (17).

[43]Tobin Siebers, "A Sexual Culture for People with Disabilities," in *Sex and Disability*, ed. Robert McRuer and Anna Mollow (Durham, NC: Duke University Press, 2012), 39.

[44]Seibers, "A Sexual Culture for People with Disabilities," 44.

rooms for the purpose of intimacy, and often have roommates.[45] In other situations a couple may need a third party to assist the active pair in their encounter, both "in the preparation for and the performance of sexual activity," something noted by Shane Clifton in his consideration of sex and the good life through a lens of virtue ethics.[46] These are all occasions where sexual intimacy falls outside typical "normative" framings of "acceptable" sexual practice— situations more likely to be deemed "deviant": sex with a third party present, sex with the perpetual chance of being interrupted or "caught," body parts used in non-typical ways, unexpected bodily fluids to navigate with catheters and colonoscopy bags, and so on.[47]

Disability activist Anne Finger stresses the importance of attention to the sexuality of people with disabilities, explaining that "sexuality is often the source of our deepest oppression; it is often the source of our deepest pain."[48] Similarly, disabled feminist Liz Crow argues that sexuality may be the most urgent battle for disability civil rights. She says that while it is "the one area above all others to have been ignored," it is also "at the absolute core of what we're working for."[49] Though she recognizes that all the rights activists seek—"employment, education, housing, transportation, etc."—are interwoven, she sees sexuality as the one that is closest to "the essence of self," where we are persons together with persons.[50]

In a culture where "the preference for ability" already "permeates nearly every" aspect of life, it is actually the realm of sexuality that, according to Tobin Seibers, may be the most "privileged domain of ability." He explains, "Sex is the action by which most people believe that ability is reproduced, by which humanity

---

[45]Abby Wilkerson, "Disability, Sex Radicalism, and Political Agency," in *Feminist Disability Studies*, ed. Kim Q. Hall (Bloomington, IN: Indiana University Press, 2011): 194–217.

[46]Shane Clifton explains, "Personal care might even be needed in preparation for and performance of sexual activity" Shane Clifton, *Crippled Grace: Disability, Virtue Ethics, and the Good Life* (Waco, TX: Baylor University Press, 2019), (162).

[47]For a conversation on these complexities, see Leah Lakshmi Piepza-Samarasinha, *Care Work: Dreaming Disability Justice* (Vancouver: Arsenal Pulp Press, 2018).

[48]Anne Finger, "Forbidden Fruit," *New Internationalist* (July 5, 1992), https://new int.org/features/1992/07/05/fruit (accessed October 18, 2022).

[49]Liz Crow, "Rippling Raspberries: Disabled Women and Sexuality," unpublished MSc dissertation, London, South Bank Polytechnic, p. 9. Quoted by Tom Shakespeare, "Disabled Sexuality: Toward Rights and Recognition," *Sexuality and Disability* 18 (3) (2000), 165.

[50]Crow, "Rippling Raspberries," 9. Quoted by Shakespeare, "Disabled Sexuality," 165.

supposedly asserts its future."[51] Thus it is particularly that ability
to reproduce through vaginal intercourse (without assistance) that
"marks sexuality as a privileged index of human ability."[52] Thus,
he asserts that in the ableist imagination it is "sex that bestows
human status." In fact, "the ideology of ability underlies the
imperative to reproduce at many levels, establishing whether an
individual supposedly represents a quality human being."[53] To be
virile or fertile becomes the mark of full humanity and to fail in
this regard is to "fail as a human being."[54] He explains that while
"successful reproduction is thought to pass our essential abilities
and qualities to our children," the reproduction of people with
disabilities is often regarded by the nondisabled and the medical
field as just another pathology to be fixed.[55] Denied their sexuality
by dominant culture, people with disabilities are also subjected
to forced sterilizations and forced abortions, penalized for
marriage, and castigated for producing children.[56] Further, while
calling for attention to be given to the sexual desire and intimate
relationships of people with disabilities, authors and activists also
note the particular precarity of people with disabilities to sexual
exploitation and assault, especially when housed in institutions.
On one hand, people with disabilities are denied sexual expression
or deemed nonsexual, and on the other, people with disabilities,
especially women with intellectual or developmental disabilities,
endure high rates of sexual abuse.[57]

Shane Clifton is among the few theologians of disability to
address sexuality.[58] He confronts the heteropatriarchal assumptions
around sex we've discussed, but from the particular perspective

---

[51]Seibers, "A Sexual Culture for People with Disabilities," 40–1.

[52]By interrogating the emphasis on reproductive sex, disability studies shares much
in common with queer theory.

[53]Seibers," A Sexual Culture for People with Disabilities," 41.

[54]Seibers, "A Sexual Culture for People with Disabilities," 41.

[55]Seibers, "A Sexual Culture for People with Disabilities," 41.

[56]See again Anne Finger who tells the story of news anchor Bree Walker whose
pregnancies were debated publicly on radio shows because her children had a
50 percent chance of inheriting ectrodactyly. Finger, "Forbidden Fruit."

[57]Eli Clare has written a moving memoire that includes his experience of sexual
abuse, as has Leah Lakshmi Piepza-Samarasinha in Care Work. See Eli Clare, Exile
and Pride: Disability Queerness, and Liberation (Durham: Duke University Press,
2015) Reissue Edition.

[58]Clifton, Crippled Grace.

of disabled men. For one, he challenges the emphasis on male sexuality as the "potency of the penis."[59] While feminist critique of Barth and Balthasar, among others, focuses rightly on the impact of their theologies on the lives of women, Clifton reminds readers that many men are harmed by patriarchal construals of masculinity and femininity as well, something also stressed by many queer and feminist theorists. He notes a voyeuristic query from the nondisabled concerning the sexual activity of men with spinal cord injury (SCI), specifically regarding whether or not they can have sex, meaning: can the man with an SCI get an erection and can he orgasm. The focus here exposes the assumptive measure of male sexuality as penetrative initiating agents. And when masculine sexual activity is singularly attributed to a penetrating phallus, men with differing modalities of sexual engagement may be perceived as passive in the sexual encounter, feminized, or denied their sexuality outright. He explains, "even the simple act of dating can be difficult, as disabled men may struggle to meet gender role expectations, such as opening doors, hugging, initiating a kiss, and so forth. More broadly, masculinity is normally bound up with notions of independence, strength, and power, but disability is conceived of as dependency, vulnerability, and impotence."[60] Within his description, one catches the fear of the male deemed passive, or of male sexuality determined by lack, that is, assumed lack of ability to fulfill gendered expectations of initiative and penetration. His research and life experience with SCI is suggestive again of the need to reconsider passivity and activity and gendered associations of penetration and receptivity.

Althaus-Reid cleverly unveils how typical articulations of the doctrine of God could replace an advert for Viagra, with terms such as *potentia inordinata* and *actus purus*. "God is the masculine (heterosexual) powerful: never tired or without impetus, God's power is unlimited and procreative."[61] Ableist, heterosexual, and male, these images are not far from those carefully and deliberately shaped in the theologies of two of the most prominent theologians of the twentieth century (and many others as well), and the male who embodies potency and strength is portrayed as analogous to God,

---

[59]SCI raises the question, "Might there be more to male sexuality than the potency of the penis?" (Clifton, *Crippled Grace*, 161).
[60]Clifton, *Crippled Grace*, 167.
[61]Althaus-Reid, *Queer God*, 53.

the male always figured as the divine in the analogy of relation. Not only are women subordinated in this relation but so too are all who are deemed passive, physically weak, or receptive in relationship. We must reject the associations of masculinity with virility and physical prowess wherever it shows up, including within our doctrines of God.

The assumption in theologies that use analogies of relation that the divine side is a masculine impulse because it is associated with active giving (penetration) and the feminine with passive receptivity pushes many disabled men (among others) beyond the margins–to deviance; where does one fit in this binary when you don't perform the role assigned to your sex? Are you sexually deviant because of a gender-bending sex life? Does non-normative sex push one outside the markers of true humanity as some crip theories have suggested? Or can we ask with Althaus-Reid if we can conceive a God who engages in giving and receiving, outside of a procreative model, without progenitor and posterity, or outside an economy of exchange that requires generative production: "We may ask if God finds Godself at home in a culture of grace, that is of pleasure given and received in a free community, without the expectation of any sort of final product or profit."[62]

The uninterrogated heterosexual coupling behind Barth's anthropology underlies his dyads of YHWH–Israel, Father–Son, Christ–Church, and so on; his precommitment to this analogy restricts his ability to find a place for other forms of intimacy, other communal ways of being in relationship, or even for celibacy.[63] His commitment to this analogy prevented him from truly recognizing the value of human relationships outside his procreative male–female couple. Expanding beyond his limited analogy of relation is important for the many differing and meaningful ways humans experience intimacy. In their own ways numerous Crip thinkers have asked why our critical conversations and cultural and religious assumptions around sexuality singularly feature coitus. If we want to destabilize compulsory heteroableism, we need to challenge the underlying assumptions within our language of heterosexual procreative coupling, as well as seek analogies outside the erotic.

---

[62]Althaus-Reid, *Queer God*, 86. She continues, "If so, then also in cultural terms, God is a Sodomite."

[63]Faye Bodley-Dangelo, *Sexual Difference, Gender, and Agency in Karl Barth's Church Dogmatics* (London: T&T Clark, 2021), 238. Also, Adrian Thatcher, *Gender and Christian Ethics* (Cambridge: Cambridge University Press, 2021), 85.

Tobin Seibers and others ask why our discussions of sexuality must be limited to reproductive sex or genital sensation. For example, Anne Finger recounts the story of DeVonna Cervantes who was told in a rehab facility that because she had become paraplegic she had "lost" her sexuality and her recovery would include coming to terms with this loss. Cervantes pushed back, having to convince medical professionals that her sexuality was more than genital sensation.[64] Tom Shakespeare likewise explains that "work around disabled sexuality should not be narrowly defined as a matter of sexual desire and physical entwining."[65] We have to expand our vision and our activism to include the range of human life and experience of those with disabilities. "To see sex as the whole story is to buy the message of the soap opera melodrama. Perhaps we shouldn't forget to value celibacy, and friendship, and the other parts of life."[66] Theologians too must push beyond Barth and others who find only one form of intimacy as the resource for theological discourse around relationships: be it trinitarian, Christological, ecclesiological, or anthropological.

In what follows, I will trouble the gendered identification of receptivity with women that is based in part on a flawed conception of heterosexual procreation and cultural stereotypes, and challenge the linkage of receptivity to passivity and surrender of agency. I highlight two examples: first, the work of queer theological ethicist Roberto Che Espinoza on power bottoms and second, the work of Eva Kittay on the active reception of care exhibited by persons with disabilities.

Queer Receptivity

One thinker creatively reimaging how we understand power is Roberto Che-Espinoza, whose work on the "interdependency of queer relating" provides fruitful material to reconsider the power relations assumed operative in the incarnation. With them we can lay bare the exchange of power and agency negotiated in the intimate space of giving and receiving.

Espinoza examines "the agency of the power bottom to disrupt (in productive ways)" expressions of power that stem from the

---

[64]Finger, "Forbidden Fruit."
[65]Shakespeare, "Disabled Sexuality," 166.
[66]Shakespeare, "Disabled Sexuality," 165.

sadism associated with colonizing hierarchies (institutions). They identify bottom space as the "margins of the margins" and draw our attention to the power and agency generated there, a power they describe as a "birthing"; it is productive. They write, "When the bottom acknowledges that the margins of the margins are the places where they are able to harness their own power, they meet the power of the dominant, not in oppositional ways, but in productive ways." They explain that the power bottom is not "necessarily overly passive ..., nor do they give up their own inherent power residing in them."[67] In fact, this reorienting of power that Espinoza describes "also demands a particular submission by those who occupy top-space."[68]

While the bottom's power stems from that space on the margins of the margins, it is enlivened in the intimate space shared by both bottom and top, which Espinoza describes as "a kaleidoscope of becoming," or a "becoming power."[69] This power is generated in the creative negotiations of agency and intimacy; it is shared, exchanged, and enjoyed in the consensual play of desire. This process cultivates "a productive power," that is "a mutual sharing of power," and "results in power being with both bottom and top."[70]

The "nexus of power and agency" described by Espinoza disturbs the hard-and-fast binary often assumed in such an encounter.[71] They weave together a portrait of power that is discovered within power exchange but motivated by the agency of the bottom. This power is neither unidirectional (top-down) nor unilateral, and is much closer to the power I see in the Logos, whose identity as divine receptivity is pure relation, and forges a creative power in intimacy, in the willing reception of the nature and activity of the human of the union. To speak of the receptivity of the Logos in Christ is not to suggest a passive sublimation of the divine by the human nature. It is not simply to switch the divine-human roles in the same

---

[67]Robyn Henderson-Espinoza, "Decolonial Erotics: Power Bottoms, Topping from Bottom Space, and the Emergence of a Queer Sexual Theology," *Feminist Theology* 26 (3) (2018). They describe a passivity of power bottoms that is rooted in agency, calling it "radical passivity" (293). Published under the above name. This scholar's name is now Roberto Che Espinoza.

[68]Henderson-Espinoza, "Decolonial Erotics," 292–3.

[69]Henderson-Espinoza, "Decolonial Erotics," 291.

[70]Henderson-Espinoza, "Decolonial Erotics," 294.

[71]Henderson-Espinoza, "Decolonial Erotics," 292.

power binary where power and agency are held by one and denied the other.

I'm drawn to Espinoza's work here, in part because they have not rejected relations that include receptivity, but have taken that relationship outside of the heterosexual framework. Clifton's description of sexuality likewise indicates the emergence of new sexualities that have some similarities with that described by Espinoza. Clifton writes, "SCI renders people more or less inert, and the higher the level of injury, the more passive a person becomes—at least at first glance."[72] When he says those with SCI may appear "at first glance" to be passive, he suggests that once we recognize sexuality beyond the parameters of heteroableist patriarchal norms, one discovers the various ways individuals express and live into intimate and sexual relationships. Clifton explains, "Studies of men reveal the potential for the emergence of a ... creative reawakening. ... This is because SCI orients a person to focus on their partners' pleasure—to enjoy the thrill of giving sexual delight. This giving is achieved inventively... by learning to be creative with the disabled body."[73] Clifton's description rejects the normative fixation on male penetration and orgasm as the threshold for sex and offers an expansive interpretation of sexuality and the body's function in sexual intimacy. Disability sexuality can offer the opportunity to explore a spectrum of eroticism and forms of union. Clifton additionally suggests that an asymmetry does not quash the potential for a mutually pleasurable intimacy and flourishing relationship. The expression and reception of intimacy and pleasure are not measured and do not presume an equivalency of exchange.

Reception of Care

My second example comes from philosopher Eva Kittay who explores the agency of recipients of care, inspired by life with her daughter Sesha, who has significant intellectual and physical disabilities. Kittay describes a form of care that requires subjectivity within the relation, for both the caregiver and the receiver of

---

[72]Clifton, *Crippled Grace*, 161.
[73]Clifton, *Crippled Grace*, 162.

care, cautioning against the "collapse of relationality" when this subjectivity is not preserved. It is this relation of two subjects that creates space for true care. The caregiver is at risk of losing self or subjectivity, because caregiving is an undervalued and often invisible role, that is too often assigned exclusively to women, who are likewise subjected to compulsory self-sacrifice for the one in their care based on social and religious expectations. Another risk is when a caregiver imposes their will upon the one receiving care, ignoring the agency of the recipient. Both the loss of self in sacrifice to care and the lack of recognition of the subjectivity of the other in the imposition of care result in the collapse of relationality, which is the space of care.

Kittay argues that in order for care to truly be "care" it must meet certain requirements. First, the one offering care must do so in good will.[74] "Care is not something we do to someone. It is something we do *for* another's benefit."[75] Care must be given with some amount of competence. And crucial for our discussion today, it is also not "care" unless it is completed through the reception of the care. Her insight here draws from her experience offering care to her 92-year-old mother, who would accept the care at times, but more often meet it with resistance. She came to realize that her daughter, who needs substantial care, would typically receive the care they gave her with grace but could also refuse and resist in her own ways. She came to see that Sesha was "much less passive" than she had acknowledged, and that even those who require much care, even for basic survival, have some power—they can refuse, resist, or fight the care offered, or they can take up the care as care, completing it in their reception.[76] Care is not care if it is imposed or forced. To qualify as "care" it must be received as such. Receptivity with disability may look to some like a dependency lacking in agency, but in terms of care, there is an exchange of power; there is the offering and there is its taking up.

Kittay also reminds us of the role of receptivity within the independence movement of disability activism, as one's independence is simultaneously dependent on caregivers, assistants, and a network of support who make that "independence" possible. Here

---

[74]Eva Kittay, *Learning from My Daughter: The Value and Care of Disabled Minds* (Oxford: Oxford University Press, 2019), 185.
[75]Kittay, *Learning from My Daughter*, 186.
[76]Kittay, *Learning from My Daughter*, 186.

independence is redefined to encompass, and thus obscure, the vast networks of assistance and provision required. She asks why elevate independence as a value in the first place: "Self-sufficiency is always a lie, whether or not we are disabled."[77] She criticizes those who dissemble independence, erasing the dependencies and relations that sustain it and thus denigrate the lives of dependents who cannot keep up the ruse. And of course, this is true for all human life; society is a web of interdependencies. She writes, "A truly independent life— one in which we need no one and no one needs us—would be a very impoverished one, even if it were possible."[78]

Kittay also provides an important consideration of the impact of feminist emphasis on certain understandings of equality as mutuality.[79] She writes, "any idea of equality that is located in the autonomous, free, and self-sufficient individual, who joins only with similarly situated others, does not easily recognize the dependency that has so occupied women's lives. By failing to recognize this dependency, such conceptions of equality effectively exclude women."[80] She explains that this mutuality doesn't apply to mothering those with extensive need and dependency such as Sesha. The parent–child relationship, like that with Sesha, can never be forced into a frame of reciprocity in a "mutual equal relationship."[81]

But this relationship of care does not mean, for Kittay, that she has to "acquiesce to the 'feminine' virtues of self-effacing self-sacrifice."[82] Rather, "it means that we need a reconfiguration of how reciprocation comes to be possible in the case of dependency work."[83] While the image of mutuality and interdependence among

---

[77]Kittay, *Learning from My Daughter*, 161.
[78]Kittay, *Learning from My Daughter*, 161.
[79]Kittay explains:

> But even feminists who have directed us away from the atomistic individualism of much traditional Western philosophy have failed to recognize the full implications of dependency. Lorraine Code, for example, acknowledging that women can achieve satisfactory relationships with both children and men, just as one can with feminist friends and colleagues, insists that equality is a crucial value. "It is a matter of mutuality." (Code 198, 56). Eva Kittay, *Loves Labor: Essays on Women, Equality, and Dependency* (New York: Routledge, 1999), 180.

[80]Kittay, *Love's Labor*, 182.
[81]Kittay, *Love's Labor*, 182.
[82]Kittay, *Love's Labor*, 180.
[83]Kittay, *Love's Labor*, 180.

persons is important for vast forms of relationality, it isn't the only way relationships and intimacy can function in a meaningful, valuable way. For Kittay, "life with Sesha underscores that there are moments when we are not 'inter'dependent. We are simply dependent and *cannot* reciprocate."[84] Much disability theology, including what I am developing here, places value on forms of interdependency for human life and for the triune life, typically by way of a perichoresis of the divine being, pouring out life to the others and receiving life from the others. This perichoresis sounds fully symmetrical and reciprocal. Covenant ontology shifts this emphasis as there is vulnerability across the life of God and some forms of dependency, but it is not an equal mode of receptivity or reliance on another.

Disability discourse demonstrates that mutuality is not always symmetrical. Some people require more help than others, even as they exist in webs of care and mutual giving; it may not always be an equal exchange. However, like Kittay emphasizes, as long as this web of care means that the needs of the caregiver are also met by another, this arrangement does not mean self-abnegation and a deleterious self-sacrifice. Kittay explains that the elevation of equality as full participation in the economic, social, or political order means someone giving substantial care for a dependent can't fully participate as an equal, unless, someone simultaneously meets her needs as well. She says, "Life with Sesha has then brought to consciousness the way in which the 'equal' portion of the formula cannot be met for the mothering person of a truly dependent individual unless the wider society provides resources for caring not only for the dependent, but also for the one who provides the care."[85] She continues, "To have one's needs met as one meets the needs of another may not be a feature of the relation between independent persons who have an equal status. Nonetheless it becomes the condition for equality for all those within a relationship of dependency, where someone is significantly and inevitably dependent on another for basic needs."[86]

This asymmetrical relationship, however, doesn't mean that the dependent one is not also a giver of gifts. Kittay acknowledges herself as a recipient of Sesha's giving as well. She calls the lessons

---

[84]Kittay, *Love's Labor*, 180.
[85]Kittay, *Love's Labor*, 181.
[86]Kittay, *Love's Labor*, 181.

she's recorded in her book *Love's Labor* the direct "product of Sesha's gentle tutoring" of her. She says, "I will continue to learn from my daughter, from those who share her mothering with me, and from ... this remarkable relationship with an exquisite person we call Sesha." And these are lessons, she says, that she will continue to receive as long as she and Sesha "have each other."[87] I appreciate Kittay's insistence on thinking of these relations outside an utterly equal exchange, outside symmetrical equivalency, for individuals to rightly relate with each other. I see something similar suggested by Espinoza: a relation beyond measurable exchange and quantifiable amounts of gift given with requisite equal measures in mutual return.

Conclusion

The cultural assumption is that to be a recipient is to be passive; only resistance in this relation could mark agency, but this is mistaken. To receive care can itself be an active willingness to be helped and to embrace the relationship that care establishes. Receptivity to care empowers—both in the sense of the "independent" living of people with disabilities and also through the assistance that families receive from other caregivers of their loved ones and the needs of caregivers met by others. Receptivity to care then enables life, if that receptivity is met with loving, non-violent, and non-dominating care. Receptivity is a form of vulnerability, but not sheer vulnerability. It should not inherently imply powerlessness or suggest lack of agency. Likewise when we think about the divine nature of Christ as existing in the mode of receptivity, this does not mean the Son lacks power, but it does suggest a different form of power, one that destabilizes the logic of dominance, a power quickened through interdependency. The divine reception of the human animates the union that is Jesus, which in turn, according to the Christian faith, provides abundant life for all.

I am not saying: we need to accept asymmetrical relations of dependency and vulnerability in a context of care and intimacy, so let's project that into God. Instead I've offered a Christological account based on the revelation of God in Christ that happens to

---

[87]Kittay, *Love's Labor*, 181.

also illuminate the value of lives in need of care, of dependence, of the potential for asymmetrical lives of care and giving, and found analogies to help illustrate trinitarian life and the hypostatic union, drawing from outside the normative accounts of nondisabled heterosexual procreative relations. I've illustrated how heterosexism and heteronormativity impact contemporary understandings of God and Christ, and how the binary upon which they rest falsely identifies receptivity as a strictly feminine principle. I've worked to disentangle the gendered attribution of the binaries underlying much theological construction while also not devaluing the lives of those who receive much care. I've offered some ideas for how we can think about the nature of Christ outside the typical framing of power, one that doesn't divinize power as dominance, but allows for receptivity and need within the Trinity and Christ. The Logos in a mode of receptivity, a posture with power and agency generated in intimacy, assumes the utterly relational identity of the second "person," who eternally exists as one who generates power in the margins of the margins, enlivened in the reception of the other. Through this shift in our conception of the nature of God in Christ we may more readily recognize the agency and power in the margins of the margins, among those devalued by prevailing social and economic measures, and we may embrace the interdependency of human life and value those who give care and those who take it up.

5

Disability and Resurrection

Introduction

Throughout this book I have endeavored to amplify Eiesland's groundbreaking work in *The Disabled God*, providing additional theological support for her assertation that God may be considered disabled because of the wounds on Jesus' resurrected body. I have built a case for an identity of the Son that is shaped eternally by and for the impaired body of Jesus, and constituted for receptivity. This understanding of the triune nature of God means that need, vulnerability, and dependency are not foreign to the being of God, and this proposal strongly resists the tendency in theology to divinize independence and autonomy as supreme values attributed to God. However, I have not attended to what is likely Eiesland's most lasting contribution to theology: her insistence that because Jesus retained his wounds, people with impairments will also retain their particular embodiments eschatologically; the resurrected life will include disabled bodies. According to Eiesland this means that "resurrection is not about the negation or erasure of our disabled bodies in hopes of perfect images, untouched by physical disability; rather Christ's resurrection offers hope that our nonconventional, and sometimes difficult, bodies participate fully in the *imago Dei* and that God is ... touched by our experience."[1] In this final chapter, I will briefly consider the history of theological speculation around the resurrected body, challenge Eiesland's emphasis on retaining an identity category of "disability" in our conceptions of the resurrected life, and propose an understanding

---

[1]Eiesland, *The Disabled God*, 107.

of eschatological life that is one of becoming that includes the body and soul in the journey of transformation.[2] In the Christian life and our eschatological hope, we understand ourselves to be grafted into the body of Christ, which means we receive his broken flesh and receive his covenant identity, an identity inflected by need, an identity formed in communal life.

Imagined Futures and Present Hope

Historians find that an insistence on a resurrected body in Jewish and Christian communities has typically corresponded with experiences of social marginalization and persecution. The claim that bodies are restored at the resurrection can function as a means of resistance to the forces that control and enact violence on marginalized and oppressed bodies.[3] One could certainly interpret Nancy Eiesland's famous assertion that disabilities are retained in heaven in this light. Her claim that impaired bodies enter resurrected life as in this life (but without pain) is a refusal of the compulsory able-bodied hegemony of our culture and much Christian teaching. Her insistence implicitly denies those ableist ideologies of acceptable modalities that oppress through access barriers and medicalized manipulation, and through the emotional or psychological violence of stigma and exclusion. Eiesland contends she doesn't need to be fixed, not now, and not in the age to come. Sharon Betcher states similarly: "[P]ersons with disabilities constitute the refusal of not only the American ideal, but Christian eschatological idealism: We refuse to be resolved, saved, made whole, thereby 'invalidating' eschatological idealism and hopefully some of the aggressive pity, preferring our histories of flesh, even as functionally enabled by technology."[4]

---

[2]Portions of this chapter were published as Lisa D. Powell, "Disability and Resurrection: Eschatological Bodies, Identity, and Continuity," *Journal of the Society of Christian Ethics* 41 (1) (Spring/Summer 2021): 89–106.

[3]Candida Moss, *Divine Bodies: Resurrecting Perfection in the New Testament and Early Christianity* (New Haven, CT: Yale University Press, 2019), 7.

[4]Sharon Betcher, "Monstrosities, Miracles, and Mission: Religion and the Politics of Disablement," in *Postcolonial Theologies: Divinity and Empire*, ed. Catherine Keller, Michael Nausner, and Mayra Rivera (St. Louis, MO: Chalice Press, 2004), 99.

Eiesland's proposal, though influential and groundbreaking, has faced critiques even from within disability theology as discussed in Chapter 1. She may have a tendency to celebrate disability to the extent that those whose relationship to their impairment differ from her positive assessment don't find room for their experience in her account. Some people with disabilities may not want that impairment for eternity; it may be painful, or related to trauma, or make basic life tasks terribly difficult. A degenerative condition, an accident, or age can change a person's embodiment such that they'd rather envision a future where they were as they were before. Eiesland is also critiqued for limiting her work explicitly to physical disabilities. Thus, as I imagine alongside her work, I aim to provide an account of the eschatological life that honors disabled bodies and minds, a future vision that doesn't erase impairment in a compulsory able-bodied Edenic restoration, but also doesn't naively romanticize impairment to elide the presence of struggle or trauma.

Eiesland places her finger directly on the wound inflicted by the eschatological musings of much Western thought. She recounts the ways in which the churches of her adolescence perpetually communicated to her that her body was not acceptable. One way this message becomes ingrained is through the infantilizing tones of nondisabled church goers promising a future body that is "normal." Eiesland gives voice to a particular experience shared by many with disabilities, that of nondisabled people assuming it is a kindness to project a future in which disability ceases to exist. Why must Christians assure people in wheelchairs or with limited mobility that someday they will run to Jesus when they could just as easily wheel there? Eiesland's work is a protest against the eschatologies that feed these encounters with well-meaning Christians, whose conception of heaven utterly erase her lived reality, objectify her body, and deny her abundant life with her wheelchair.

Alison Kafer describes a similar relationship between how one views disability and the sort of future one envisions for people with impairments. When an act of arson at her apartment building resulted in the amputation of both of her legs and profound scarring on her body, Kafer endured the pity of those around her who could imagine only a lonely and tragic future for her. However, this was not the only future projected for her. Her encounters with other persons living with disabilities gave her "stories of lives lived fully," and she writes, "my future according to them, involves not isolation and pathos but community and possibility."[5] One perspective construes disability as a "tragedy that effectively prevents one from leading a good life," while the other identifies ableism, and not disability, as the barrier to future happiness.[6] Though coming from different places and with very different outcomes, both outlooks demonstrate a similar logic: "How one understands disability in the present determines how one imagines disability in the future; one's assumptions about the experience of disability create one's conception of a better future."[7] Kafer's description of the futures imagined through the ableist lens could just as easily be an account of a typical Christian eschatological vision. She writes, "A better future ... is one that excludes disability and disabled bodies; indeed, it is the very *absence* of disability that signals this better future."[8] This presumptive desire for a disability-free future is assumed as self-evident, and no value is recognized in a future that includes people with disabilities.[9] Kafer rejects this as a failure of imagination. "Rather than assume that a 'good' future naturally and obviously depends upon the eradication of disability, we must recognize this perspective as colored by histories of ableism and disability oppression."[10]

According to Kafer the imagined futures of persons with disabilities impact their present prospects, either through stigmatization and pity or in creative possibilities and fulfillment. Her attention to this future has deep resonance with the work of Eiesland, who likewise noted that the way we talk about the future of disabled bodies impacts the way people are treated in the present, and the opportunities, supports, and access available today. These aren't insignificant musings: what we envision regarding the future communicates what we consider to be lives worth living. In imagining more accessible futures, Kafer says she is "yearning for an elsewhere—and perhaps, an 'elsewhen'—in which disability is understood ... as political, as valuable, as integral."[11] What follows is an exercise in this work of imagining such an "elsewhen."

---

[5]Kafer, *Feminist, Queer, Crip*, 2.
[6]Kafer, *Feminist, Queer, Crip*, 2.
[7]Kafer, *Feminist, Queer, Crip*, 2.
[8]Kafer, *Feminist, Queer, Crip*, 2.
[9]Kafer, *Feminist, Queer, Crip*, 3.
[10]Kafer, *Feminist, Queer, Crip*, 3.
[11]Kafer, *Feminist, Queer, Crip*, 3. She admits this is tricky ground. She finds it "absolutely essential to dismantle the purposed self evidence" of the claim: "A future

Eschatological Speculation and the Resurrected Body

The image of the resurrected body as perfected in its embodiment of a particular ideal is rooted in a long history of theological speculation. Some early theologians assumed everyone's resurrected body appeared to be the age of thirty, including those who died in infancy and those in old age, because that was the age assumed for the resurrected Christ, the "first fruits" of resurrection, but also because this was considered the peak of human development at the time.[12] Jesus' retained wounds, however, drew few to conclude we retain bodily impairments beyond a few reflections on wounds obtained in acts of faith. Augustine, for example, argued that martyrs would retain beautified scars with severed limbs reattached at glorified seams, all as signs of their virtue.[13] Likewise Gregory of Nyssa claimed his sister Macrina would keep the scar from a tumor on her chest that was miraculously healed to demonstrate God's power in the everlasting life.[14] A peculiar tradition around the veneration of Jesus' foreskin, also raised a conundrum, as its earthly persistence suggests parts of the body lost on earth aren't restored to the eschatological person after all, leaving open the possibility that other severed body parts remain behind, unrestored, and unglorified.[15] Thus, a number of theologians insisted the foreskin was restored to Jesus' resurrected body "so that he would

---

with disability is a future no one wants," yet she recognizes there is truth in it, even from her own experience. She does not, for example, wish to be future impaired. "I realize that position is itself marked by an ableist failure of imagination, but I can't deny holding it" (4).

[12]Augustine was consistent on his assertion that we rise with our sexed bodies, but not on the age. Ephraim, however, boldly asserted that babies will rise as adults and recognize their parents and vice versa. See Caroline Walker Bynum, *The Resurrection of the Body in Western Christianity, 200–1336* (New York City: Columbia University Press, 1994), 76–7. Peter Lombard similarly claims all rise the same age but not the same stature. Each will receive the stature he had (or would have had) in youth (122). Thomas Aquinas also asserts this (265).

[13]Saint Augustine, *City of God*, trans. D. D. Marcus Dodds (New York: Random House, 1993), Modern Library Edition, XXII.19. Bonaventure also said that the scars of the martyrs will remain as "signs of merit and triumph" (see Bynum, *The Resurrection of the Body*, 254).

[14]Gregory of Nyssa, *The Life of Macrina*.

[15]Moss, *Divine Bodies*, 1.

be perfect in every respect, even this. For we too at the general resurrection will receive back our bodies perfected."[16]

Most theologians agreed that all impairments are not only corrected or healed, but resurrected bodies also appear without blemish, with an emphasis on beauty and symmetry reflecting the cultural ideals of their day. Augustine even claimed that all men will have beards in heaven because they must rise as handsome as possible.[17] Bonaventure likewise claimed that the "elect will rise with all deformities corrected," but he asserted that some deformities will rise with evil individuals for damnation because "God will not give to the evil any beauty they lacked on earth."[18] Yet, recognizability and continuity of identity remained important for most theologians, so for Bonaventure the elect will "rise perfect and beautiful" but will retain individual particularities, such as stature, sex, and body size.[19] Tertullian used the idea of the resurrection of the body to caution against gluttony, specifying that a thin person will find it easier to get through the narrow gate into heaven.[20] This projection of sociocultural values into the resurrected life is an unfortunate feature of much early theological thought around the resurrection and our expected embodiment.

Affirmation of the material continuity of the body was a safeguard to the continuity of identity, between who we understand ourselves to be in this world and that to come. For example, Caroline Walker Bynum argues persuasively that even those debates most trivial and obscure to modern readers, such as whether every inch of hair and nails cut in the course of one's life are returned to your body at the resurrection, are rooted in anxiety around identity in the resurrected life.[21] However, Bynum has also well documented that the insistence among some theologians that our bodies retain identifying physical features serves their underlying commitment to the preservation of social hierarchies in heaven, especially the ordering of the sexes. For example, Jerome, Tertullian, and Augustine, among others, explicitly

---

[16]The Blessed Theophylact, Archbishop of Ohrid and Bulgaria, "Chapter 2:21-27," *The Explanation of the Gospel of Luke*, trans. Christopher Stade (House Springs, MO: Chrysostom Press, 1997), 33.

[17]Bynum, *The Resurrection of the Body*, 99.

[18]Bynum, *The Resurrection of the Body*, 254.

[19]Bynum, *The Resurrection of the Body*, 254.

[20]Tertullian, *De ieiundio*, ch. 17, pp. 1276–7; see also ch. 12, pp. 1270–1. Bynum, *The Resurrection of the Body*, 40.

[21]Bynum, *Fragmentation and Redemption: Essays on Gender and the Human Body in Medieval Religion* (New York: Zone Books, 1992), 266–97.

assert there will be "rank and hierarchy in heaven," and for some, at least one's sex must be identifiable to facilitate such an ordering.[22] In fact, Jerome mused that if we don't retain our distinguishable sexes, that is, genitals, then the virgin and the repentant prostitute would appear as equals, which was unacceptable.[23]

What is undesirable, or rather what is most feared in a particular social context, shapes the imaginations of theologians; historically this appears as a fear of decay, of impairment, and of loss of status or rank (a fear that all will be equal).[24] Though our modern fears share much in common with these, more precisely in late capitalist societies we fear dependency and loss of productivity, and our eschatological visions glorify notions of independence and self-sufficiency.

Yet these speculations also stem from a series of interrelated theological claims that include the notion of an original perfect embodiment in Eden that is tragically lost in the Fall, leading to the possibility of impairment and illness. Accordingly, the glorified body will be a perfection of Edenic bodies, imaged in ways that fulfill the cultural expectations of beauty, typically youthful, handsome, athletic, and able-bodied. Eiesland's insistence that the disabled body retains these marks of impairment into the resurrected life denies that original humanity was created to be free of impairment, that impairments are a result of sin entering the world, and that the reign of God necessarily means a perfection of that supposed original plan. If impairments aren't the result of sin, if they don't fall outside of God's original creation, then why wouldn't they be welcomed into the resurrected community?

Identity in Contemporary Liberation Theology

Though the traditions' insistence on real material continuity grows out of a belief that the material of Jesus' earthly body was

---

[22]Bynum, *Resurrection of the Body*, 100; Augustine, Sermon 132, ch. 3, para. 3 (quoted in Bynum).

[23]Bynum, *Resurrection of the Body*, 90–1. Jerome also had a ranking of the chaste over the married extended in the resurrected life, facilitated by the retaining of visible sexes (genitals).

[24]Bynum, *Resurrection of the Body*, 90–1.

resurrected (signified by the wounds and the empty tomb), the vehemence with which it was stressed stems from the conviction that our bodies are integral to our identities, so much so that our souls cannot be perfected without them. I do not want to deny the vital relationship between body and identity, quite the contrary, but we have good reason to interrogate a strict continuity of identity rooted in recognizable bodies. First, Christian insistence on this matter masks an allegiance to sociocultural hierarchies. Second, these identities are shaped in part by the meaning given to our bodies by a sociocultural system that is white supremacist, ableist, and heteropatriarchal. Most contemporary theologians would agree that our discourse around the resurrected life should not be shaped by a precommitment to social hierarchies tied to efforts to protect power and should not be based on cultural and social valuations of differing embodiments, be it the ranking of value based on race, sex, ability, or the like. But how do we account for identities that are forged within a sociocultural matrix that rewards and punishes based on one's particular embodiment, identities shaped at least in part by social pressures and norms that cast persons against structures of power that bruise or embrace, depending on your body, your affect, your gait, or your embodied performance? To what extent are our bodies given meaning by the forces of heteropatriarchal, ableist white supremacy that inform our identity-shaping experiences? And what do we make of these body-identities as they are understood to persist eternally through the resurrection? Surely, for many on the underside of this system, the hoped-for kingdom includes a radical discontinuity from the sociocultural world we currently inhabit, including the identities it assigns. How do we understand a continuity of identity that simultaneously evacuates fixed identity categories that are constructed in this noxious sociocultural matrix?

Those whose bodies are scrutinized, surveilled, devalued, and targeted for violence and abuse have contributed most significantly to contemporary understandings of the role our bodies have in the formation of our identities. And a number of liberation theologians and ethicists are questioning the ways in which identity is then deployed in the service of liberative efforts. They ask what benefit our use of those identity categories offers when they were invented for the purpose of economic and political exploitation and power. For example, queer theological ethics interrogates the binaries and concomitant impulse toward classification, division, and valuation typical of Western thought and foundational to constructed identity categories. Brandy Daniels summarizes this emphasis: "Queer theory challenges the fixed nature of identity, recognizing identity as historically and socially shaped by various forces of power—and that freedom (political, social, or otherwise) lies in challenging and resisting the notion of fixed identity."[25] Queer theory insists that the categories of sex, gender, and sexuality are neither binary nor natural; they are neither necessary nor given; they are forged in history. Queer theory rejects the impulse toward stable categories altogether in an effort to create openings for the fluidity of human embodiments, expressions, and sexualities as it embraces the multiplicities of becoming.

We find similar challenges raised by theologians on race. For example, Jonathan Tran in *Asian Americans and the Spirit of Racial Capitalism* questions the preoccupation with identity in much antiracist work because it reinforces racialization by drawing from the categories of racial identity that were originally determined by white supremacy, which explains why it is also unable to adequately account for race outside the white/Black binary. Contrary to the efforts of what Trans calls "antiracist orthodoxy," he argues that "racial identity cannot be so easily appropriated."[26] Race becomes a category that elides the economic exploitation which was the purpose for racializing in the first place. It functions within capitalism for the advancement of white wealth: "to be racialized is … to be commodified."[27] Racial identity cannot be simply taken up and utilized for another purpose without participating in the system that created it, because it was strategically "invented for the sake of exercising the social control necessary for sustained economic exploitation and domination."[28] Thus Tran charges that "embracing racial identities that come downstream from racialization amounts to an intimate embrace of the political economy that produced them."[29] One must denounce the economic structure that invented race and deploys it, instead of trying to co-opt the categories this

---

[25]Brandy Daniels, "Queer Theory," in *Religion: Embodied Religion*, ed. Kent Brintall (New York: Macmillan Reference, 2016), 296.

[26]Jonathan Tran, *Asian Americans and the Spirit of Racial Capitalism* (Oxford: Oxford University Press, 2022), 11.

[27]Tran, *Asian Americans*, 13.

[28]Tran, *Asian Americans*, 79.

[29]Tran, *Asian Americans*, 9–10.

system erected. In opposition to racial capitalism Tran posits the divine economy, or "deep economy," predicated on the absolute value of God. Rather than racial identity as the grounding of antiracist work, he proposes deracialized identities formed in particular doxological practices in community.

From the field of systematic theology, J. Kameron Carter argues in *Race: A Theological Account*, that blackness is a category created by whiteness, and so proposes exiting these categories altogether as we forge new identities through the covenant into which we are grafted through the Jewish flesh of Jesus. He writes, "black liberation theology's attempt ... to salvage the blackness that modernity has constructed by converting it into a site of cultural power ... is not radical enough. This is because it ironically leaves whiteness in place .... [W]hat is needed is an understanding of Christian existence as ever-grounded in the Jewish, nonracial flesh of Jesus and thus as an articulation of the *covenantal* life of Israel."[30]

Carter specifies the meaning for Christianity of Jesus' Jewishness by tracing his legacy back to Abram's call to leave Ur and his family of origin. Abram ventures out on a journey, abandoning "the identity that Ur assigned to him in order eventually to be renamed Abraham. This new name indexes his identity as an identity *in relationship*" with YHWH and ultimately with this new people who will become.[31] Carter explains that Abram's "identity is not something that he constructs. It always lies ahead of him ... The ground then of his identity is his openness to YHWH's call."[32] Based upon Carter's reading of the Abrahamic narrative, Jesus stands within a people "whose identity, in being a covenantal and thus a nonracial identity, is always eschatologically in front of them. It always exceeds them."[33] Based on Carter's account, to be Christian is to be grafted into the Jewish flesh of Jesus and given that identity rooted in journey and not in arrival, and marked by openness. This allows Carter to claim that to "enter into Christ is to enter into YHWH's covenant and this entry entails leaving behind ... racialized identity. It is to exit whiteness and the identities that whiteness creates."[34] Our identities then, like Christ's own, are forged in relationship, in covenant.

---

[30]Carter, *Race*, 192.
[31]Carter, *Race*, 250–1.
[32]Carter, *Race*, 354.
[33]Carter, *Race*, 250.
[34]Carter, *Race*, 366.

Disability and Identity

A key point for Carter is that the Christian community is a people not bound to each other by familial relation, nor by race, nationality, and so on. Christians are called out of these categories to become a people together identified by the call of God and their reception of the call to leave and journey together. He understands this as an interracial identity, a mulatto identity, though he acknowledges that using this term itself works from within modern racial categories.

Carter's interpretation of Christian identity as mulatto shares striking similarity to a point often raised about disability as an atypical minority group because no necessary family resemblance exists among persons with disabilities, and the needs and experiences of persons with disabilities vary greatly, resulting in different access needs. Membership in this group is also by nature open to all ages, races, class, gender, and so on. We may all find ourselves disabled temporarily or permanently, and likely with age, we will. So, while mestizaje, mulatez, or hybridity signal an openness beyond racial/ethnic boundaries for Carter and others, disability also shares this openness, but may do still more for our understanding of eschatological identities.[35]

Sharon Betcher makes a similar claim for identity from a Crip perspective, arguing that Crip theory emphasizes a "fluidity of selfhood, embedded in evolutionary becomings."[36] She describes Crip experience as an ongoing journey of becoming that includes the body, but does not seek static identity categories defined by disability. Thus, it pushes to that radical edge Carter and Tran are also seeking, one that exits identity categories created by ableist white supremacy and toward identities marked by openness and ongoing becoming or journey. Thus eschatology also does not promise a final closed identity, but through an engrafting into Christ, an identity formed in covenant relationship and community practices.

---

[35]"There is among persons disabled, in fact, 'no necessary family resemblance,' for disability 'describes nothing shared, no one form of embodiment or orientation to the world" Betcher, "Crip/tography," 98–115, 102; quoting Petra Kuppers, "Toward a Rhizomatic Model of Disability: Poetry, Performance and Touch," *Journal of Literary & Cultural Studies* 3 (3) (2009): 228, 233.

[36]Sharon Betcher, "Crip/tography," 102.

While Carter gives some attention to the body of Christ and his suffering, the relationship of Jesus' wounded flesh to the scars on bodies grafted into his is taken up more directly by womanist theologian and ethicist M. Shawn Copeland. She considers the role of scars in our identities and attends to the scars that could be traced on the bodies of so many Black women, men, and children. One example she gives is Lavinia Bell, who was born free and stolen into slavery; after repeated attempts to escape, in addition to many whippings, the master of the plantation branded her in multiple places, cut off a finger, and slit both of her ears. Copeland writes, "The marks on her flesh identify her, tell us who she is, and bear witness to her desire and agency."[37] Copeland doesn't ignore the traumatic history of body marks, and she endeavors to carefully account for the lives and bodies of Black women who bore horrific suffering, but she reinterprets the meaning of our bodies and scars in light of one's incorporation into the life of Jesus, whose body endured traumatic wounding as well. She emphasizes physical scars, which mark violence but also evince resistance and resilience. She thus offers a way to honor these histories and their body-marks as sites of struggle, while not romanticizing or beautifying them as Augustine did for the martyrs, which would glorify the suffering they signal, but neither does her project erase them in the resurrected life, which would figure them as trivial or insignificant.

Copeland also attends to the wounds that can remain hidden in this life, such as emotional and psychological pain; these too are incorporated into the body of Christ. Eiesland also addresses this, interpreting the wound on Jesus' side as a hidden impairment, likening it to many who pass with effort and struggle as nondisabled. Copeland writes,

> The only body capable of taking us *all* in as we are with all our different body marks ... is the body of Christ. This taking us in, this in-corporation, is akin to sublation, not erasure, not uniformity: the *basileia* praxis revalues our identities and differences, even as it preserves the integrity and significance of our body marks. At the same time, those very particular body

---

[37]M. Shawn Copeland, *Enfleshing Freedom: Body, Race, and Being* (Minneapolis, MN: Fortress Press, 2009), 116.

marks are relativized, reoriented, and reappropriated under his sign, the sign of the cross. Thus, in solidarity and in love of others and the Other, we are (re)made and (re)marked as the flesh of Christ, as the flesh of his church.[38]

Differences, scars, or body marks, are not erased in Christ, but are transformed in this reevaluation and reappropriation within the reign of God.

In sum, with Carter and Copeland we consider eschatological life as one in which we are incorporated into the body of Christ. For Carter this means being grafted into the Jewish flesh of Jesus, which he reads as open and nonracial, and an identity created by relationship with a God whose call to covenant we receive. Copeland's move, though similarly emphasizing our identities as grounded in Christ, gives attention to histories of trauma, including Christ's own, and considers these scars in eschatological perspective. Yet Eiesland's interpretation of the body of Christ is somewhat different still. For her, the impaired Christ signals the interdependence of God, an ontology not "willed from a position of power," but as a "necessary condition for [God's] life."[39] She explains: "To posit a Jesus Christ who needs care and mutuality as essential to human-divine survival does not symbolize either humanity or divinity as powerless."[40] She explains that this understanding of God "debunks the myth of individualism and hierarchical orders," a myth that posits transcendence as freedom from encumbrances and not needing anyone.[41] Instead her view "constitutes the divine as somebody in relation to other bodies."[42] I argue that this is the body into which we are engrafted, the disabled Jewish flesh of Jesus, and this is the identity we receive in Christ, one forged in openness, vulnerability, covenant relationship, and interdependence.

---

[38]Copeland, *Enfleshing Freedom*, 83.
[39]Eiesland, *Disabled God*, 103. She writes: "The disabled God embodies practical interdependence, not simply willing to be interrelated from a position of power, but depending on it from a position of need."
[40]Eiesland, *Disabled God*, 103.
[41]Eiesland, *Disabled God*, 103.
[42]Eiesland, *Disabled God*, 103.

Amos Yong's Disability Eschatology

One theologian who has expanded Eiesland's proposal for resurrected impairments is Amos Yong, as he thinks about an eschatological future inclusive of those with intellectual disability.[43] Yong draws from Gregory of Nyssa's notion of *epektasis* (perfection) to shift the imagery of eschatological life away from the static perfection often associated with Augustine toward a dynamism of ongoing eternal movement toward the fullness of God. For Nyssa perfection was not the static, unchanging achievement of an ideal, but perfection becomes redefined as "never arriving," and the soul's perpetual journey. Says Nyssa, "this is truly perfection: never to stop growing towards what is better and never placing any limit on perfection."[44] The infinity of God cannot be exhausted, God cannot be fully comprehended, and thus our desire for God is never quenched. "There is always an unlimited good beyond" our current grasp or moment.[45] Yong describes this process as one in which *the body* "finds its rest in the unending process of being transformed by the glory of God in ways that overturn the binary of dichotomies not only of male/female but also of disabled/nondisabled."[46]

Yong speculates that infants will be resurrected as infants but will not remain as such, as in eternity they will continue to mature, and grow in knowledge and wisdom. He further suggests that people with Trisomy 21 (Down syndrome) will be resurrected with the phenotypical features with which they lived, ensuring the continuity with their earthly bodies and their recognizability, and

---

[43]Amos Yong's work on disability and resurrection has fueled some debate. See for example: R. T. Mullins, "Some Difficulties for Amos Yong's Disability Theology of the Resurrection," *Ars Disputandi*, (2011) 11:1, 24–32. Amos Yong responded with Amos Yong (2012) "Disability Theology of the Resurrection: Persisting Questions and Additional Considerations—A Response to Ryan Mullins," *Ars Disputandi*, 12:1, 4–10. Also James Barton Gould (2016) "The Hope of Heavenly Healing of Disability Part 1: Theological Issues," *Journal of Disability & Religion*, 20:4, 317–34. And James Barton Gould (2017) "The Hope of Heavenly Healing of Disability Part 2—Philosophical Issues," *Journal of Disability & Religion*, 21:1, 98–116.

[44]Gregory of Nyssa, "On Perfection," in *Saint Gregory of Nyssa: Ascetical Works*, trans. Virginia Callahan (Washington, DC: Catholic University Press of America, 1967), 122.

[45]Gregory of Nyssa, *Commentary on the Song of Songs*, trans. Casimir McCambley. (Brookline, MA: Hellenic College Press, 1987).

[46]Amos Yong, *Theology and Down Syndrome: Reimaging Disability in Late Modernity* (Waco, TX: Baylor University Press, 2007), 281.

will also, along with all the redeemed, grow in knowledge, love, and goodness in the unending process of theosis.[47] This notion of ongoing transformation allows Yong to assert that impaired bodies are welcomed completely into the reign of God, but that those with disabilities, like everyone else, will participate in an unending process of transformation that may mean a movement away from disabling conditions, among other things, as we grow in knowledge of God and likeness to Christ. Whereas most accounts of the soul's eschatological progress or journey focus on just that—the soul— Yong suggests that in some way our body's transformation is a part of this ongoing process of eschatological glorification that results not in the erasure of scars or marks but their transformation.

Jesus' resurrected scars are not the only biblical evidence for retained impairments. An interesting parallel to Yong's proposal is found in Candida Moss's interpretation of the Gospel of Mark, where Jesus describes amputees entering the kingdom of God and the physically beautiful or symmetrical being damned.

> If your hand causes you to stumble, cut it off; it is better for you to enter life maimed than to have two hands and to go to hell … And if your foot causes you to stumble, cut it off; it is better for you to enter life lame than to have two feet and to be thrown into hell. And if your eye causes you to stumble, tear it out; it is better for you to enter the kingdom of God with one eye than to have two eyes and to be thrown into hell.[48]

Along with at least one distinguished Marcan scholar, she interprets the gospel as indicating that amputees will enter eternal life maimed but may not remain that way.[49] The image here is of impairments received into heaven, "at least for some period of time."[50] She also includes later hagiographical accounts of the life of St. Mark to drive home her point—Mark is said to have cut off his thumb so that he could not be promoted to the priesthood, yet "the distorted

---

[47]Yong, *Theology and Down Syndrome*, 283.
[48]Mk 9:43-7. NRSV.
[49]Moss, *Divine Bodies*, 58–65. Joel Marcus, *Mark 8–16*, Anchor Yale Bible Commentary (New Haven, CT: Yale University Press, 2009), 690.
[50]Moss identifies a contrast in Mark between "deformed eternal life and normal-bodied damnation" and notes that Mark insists "that deformity enters heaven while aesthetically pleasing wholeness is cast into hell" (*Divine Bodies*, 61).

and disfigured body is still acceptable and perfect before God [as] Mark is ordained despite his missing digit."[51]

Resurrection and Radical Discontinuity

I consider Yong's vision of dynamism within our heavenly bodies an improvement upon Eiesland's brief account, as his proposal is open to the complexity of differing impairments and the diversity of experience people have with their bodies and minds. However, I want to push a little further. I want to consider how we can talk about an eschatological future with less reliance upon a notion of progress, which seems unavoidable in Yong's proposal. Does Yong's description of gaining more knowledge eternally mean a progressive attainment of intellectual ability?

I want to envision a future of transformation that allows us to retain some continuity of identity, which he does, but where the hope offered doesn't include results still rooted in our sociocultural value system, where salvation looks like gaining more knowledge. Continuity is important, but we also need radical discontinuity as so much of our self-understanding is derived through our self-assessments in light of sociocultural values and not from our incorporation into the body of Christ. Thus, there needs to be an account of some rupture with old identity categories. I see Yong moving in that direction, with his claim that the presence of God will overturn worldly binaries, but it isn't radical enough to truly disrupt the ableist imaginations at work in most Christian eschatololology. Eschatology requires our apocalyptic imagination, as resurrection inaugurates a new logic, radically beyond the structures that currently reward and punish bodies based on norms constructed for economic and political exploitation. Thus, in what follows I will argue for ongoing transformation of body-identity as one's eternal eschatological journey of becoming. I also want to explore a future envisioning that doesn't result in an eventual erasure of impairment but the undoing of ability itself as all are incorporated into the impaired body of Jesus, that is not into an identity shaped by the abled/disabled binary, but by the interdependent life of Christ.

---

[51]Moss notes that St. Mark becomes known as the healer of mangled hands (*Divine Bodies*, 64–5).

The work of theological ethicist Roberto Che Espinoza is particularly helpful here, in their development of an ontology of becoming. Drawing from trans methodologies to illustrate the movement inherent in this conception of being, they levy a powerful critique against the heterologics that permeate Christian thought, taking aim at the "overwhelming impulse to neatly categorize identities into recognizable classifications."[52] Though not explicitly referencing the resurrected life in their proposal, Espinoza targets the "*telos* of perfection and stability" associated with Enlightenment ideologies, but which we've also seen proclaimed in eschatologies and doctrines of the resurrected body from antiquity. Their transing of ontology, the understanding of one's being as open to possibility, not closed in fixed identity or static embodiment, works to support an understanding of the human that resists the supposition that fulfillment results in a static identity or a perfected and unchanging embodiment. Trans approaches to theological discourse provide a vocabulary and fuel an imagination to break with the teleologies of typical Western conceptions of resurrection.

Importantly, Espinoza proposes an ontology of becoming that includes not only gender in this open movement but our bodies themselves, which are likewise not static or fixed. They call on theology and ethics to "move … into a more creative and generative expression of the materiality of the body,"[53] emphasizing that the body "is always becoming and always becoming different from itself."[54] Even skin, as our largest organ, "is in a state of constant movement, a motion that abides in the frame of becoming."[55] Thus if we are to understand our being as always in becoming, then so too are our bodies, which the Christian tradition has long insisted are integral to our personhood. And if we insist that the resurrected body is important to personhood as it is part of the eschatological life with God, then the body too continues in that movement of becoming as part of Christian hope.[56]

---

[52]Robyn Henderson-Espinoza, "Transing Religion: Moving Beyond the Logic of the (Hetero)Norm of Binaries, *Journal of Feminist Studies in Religion* 34 (1) (Spring 2018): 88. See also Henderson-Espinoza, *Body Becoming: A Path to Our Liberation* (Minneapolis, MN: Broadleaf Books, 2022). This author now publishes under the name Roberto Che Espinoza.

[53]Henderson-Espinoza, "Transing Religion," 90.

[54]Henderson-Espinoza, "Transing Religion," 91.

[55]Henderson-Espinoza, "Transing Religion," 90.

[56]For more on resurrection in relation to queer identity see my essay Lisa D. Powell, "Resurrection and Queer Identity," in *Routledge Companion to Christian Ethics*, ed. D. Stephen Long and Rebekah L. Miles (London: Routledge, 2023), pp. 275–88.

The identities to which we cling in our hope for continuity of person (realized in our bodily integrity) are forged in a matrix of sociocultural power contrary to life in Christ. Crucial here is not only the challenge to stable identity categories shaped in and by this context, but also the attention to the ongoing becoming of the fully embodied person in the resurrected life. Thus the "discontinuous life narratives of trans folk" provide ground to imagine the radical discontinuity of resurrected life outside this matrix.[57] The nonlinear transing of identities and bodies in motion is analogous to the apocalyptic rupture and eternal transformation that must accompany our resurrection hope.

Conclusion

There is some theological consensus around the need for continuity between ourselves as known in this life and in the next, to remain recognizable to ourselves and our loved ones, but some radical discontinuity must also be a part of our eschatological hope, not only socially, as in a reign of peace, justice, and harmony, but subjectively as well. Is it simply that disabled bodies are retained in heaven, so some are disabled and some are not? Or is there a more radical new identity formed through our grafting into the body of Christ that persists in ongoing transformation throughout the eschatological future?

Application of these critiques of identity is complicated by debates within disability studies itself. While the social model of disability views disability primarily as a social construct, and thus could be seen as a category to be exited entirely, like whiteness and blackness, voices within the movement point out that it isn't only a social construct. Impairment often includes chronic pain, deep fatigue, and struggle that is not overcome through eradicating stigma or providing accommodation and access. These conditions exist regardless of the value society places on impaired bodies. Nonetheless, discourse across liberation theology and ethics suggests to me that perhaps Eiesland's vision of retained impairments in the

---

[57]Stephen D. Moore, Kent Brintnall, and Joseph Marchall, "Queer Disorientations: Four Turns and a Twist," in *Sexual Disorientations: Queer Temporalities, Affects, Theologies*, ed. Kent Brintnall, Joseph Marchall, and Stephen D. Moore (New York: Fordam University Press, 2018), 14.

eschatological life isn't radical enough. It still works within the social category constructed to enforce "normalcy." Is "disability theology" in part defined by the boundaries drawn by an ableist culture? As Lennard Davis notes, disability "like so many other [modern binary categories]—straight/gay, male/female, black/white, rich/poor—is part of an ideology of containment and a politics of power and fear."[58] Hopefully it's clear that the assertion that all people are resurrected with beautiful, symmetrical ideal bodies is unacceptable, but our vision still needs more than just an able-bodied space to which people with disabilities gain access and acceptance. How can we envision a future beyond golden streets with curb cuts and gates wide enough for all body sizes and wheelchairs? What would it mean to think about our identities outside categories of ability altogether yet still honor the bodies of persons with disabilities?

This challenge to envision radically different futures comes from within the disability justice movement itself, calling us to look for creative ways to change the framework, instead of just trying to make the frame bigger to include a wider range of bodies. For example, in recent years a popular hashtag has emerged: #disabledpeoplearehot. The hashtag is usually attached to a picture of a person with disabilities feeling and looking sexy. Mia Mingus, a leading disability justice activist, critiques such body positive movements within disability circles because rather than being revolutionary, they just disguise the same demand to be perceived as physically desirable. These affirmations, in an attempt to simply get more bodies to count as beautiful, remain situated in a framework that hales physical beauty as a supreme asset and derides corporeal ugliness with revulsion.[59] She identifies something similar in the push for independence within disability activism, which keeps in place a system that demands people be independent and productive to have social worth.[60] Instead Mingus calls for radical

---

[58]Lennard Davis, *Enforcing Normalcy: Disability, Deafness, and the Body* (London: Verso, 1995), 4.

[59]One of Mingus's most read pieces is a keynote address given in 2011, titled "Moving Toward the Ugly: A Politic Beyond Desirability." https://leavingevidence. wordpress.com/2011/08/22/moving-toward-the-ugly-a-politic-beyond-desirability/. Accessed April 24, 2020.

[60]See Mingus's essay, "Changing the Framework: Disability Justice—How Our Communities Can Move beyond Access to Wholeness," https://leavingevidence. wordpress.com/2011/02/12/changing-the-framework-disability-justice/. Accessed April 24, 2020.

interdependence, not more activism for access to able-bodied spaces and production, but a razing of the ableist structure altogether.

Debra Creamer sees a similar situation playing out in disability theology when it follows liberation movements that don't call into question the structures to which they seek access. She writes,

> we hear slogans proclaiming, "Gay is good" or "Women are strong." These claims, rather than challenging the deficit model as a whole, suggest instead that certain characteristics (gender and orientation) are not deficits as previously noted, but rather strengths or advantages ... Disability theology could make similar claims, and in fact has done so within the social/minority group model. ... This logic does not challenge the deficit model but rather narrowly claims that disability itself is not a deficit—it changes which side of the equation we are on without actually challenging the equation.[61]

Claiming disabled bodies are received into resurrected life without requiring repair was an important shift in the way we think about human destiny in God, but it doesn't do enough to disrupt the ableist underpinnings of our vision of God's reign. Our eschatological imagination is limited by our fear of dependency and loss or lack of self-sufficiency, and so our visions of God's reign, even Eiesland's to some extent, are constrained by a preservation of this particular value—we must be independent individuals. Part of the problem with the eschatological imagination of the church isn't only that it was shaped by ableist presumptions, but that these speculations on future identity reflect modern culture's celebration of self-sufficiency.

Carter and others speak of hybridity as a way of dissolving racial identification. In my proposal it signals a mixing of need and offering that dissolves the worldly glorification of ability and self-sufficiency, and creates an outpouring and an influx of care and life-giving love needed and given by each and all. With Copeland I want to see our body marks as indicative of our resilience retained without the suffering that produced them. I don't want an erasure of our histories and the relationships that constitute us, just as I don't want a Jesus who undoes his circumcision at Resurrection, erasing his place in the covenant community of Israel and his

---

[61]Creamer, *Disability and Christian Theology*, 95.

history as a 1st Century Jew. But I also desire radical discontinuity, as the demands of individuated identity give way to a communal formation of selves.

The future I envision is a celebration not of particular embodiments disabled or otherwise, but a journey into the glorification or perfection of mutual care, interdependence, and vulnerability. Perhaps this looks more like the dissolution of ability altogether. Perhaps this is participation in perichoresis. Copeland writes:

> In this body [the mystical body of Christ] each member has her or his own distinct existence; each remains herself or himself. But, even as "we remain ourselves, we do not remain our own."... Through the animation of the Spirit we are knitted and joined together; we find authentic identity in union with the Three Divine Persons and with one another.[62]

This is an identity that retains marks of resilience and resistance, of relationships and community, but grows increasingly less our own and more a complex web of mutual life together in Christ. To be grafted into the body of Christ as Carter, Copeland, and many others have considered is to be progressively less independent. This does not mean our identities become defined by absolute need, but are transformed through interwoven webs of care. With Yong, I see eschatological perfection as ever changing in that we embody Christ ever more fully, but this means we are ever growing less autonomous as our identities become communal in identification, or substantiated by relationships.

Perhaps the traditional idea that eschatological life mirrors original creation, but in its perfection and glorification, isn't so misguided after all. I would, however, read this original account differently. The natural progression of human life is from infant dependency toward aging dependency. This movement toward dependency is not a result of the Fall but a sign of the web of care and interdependent life always intended by God, which was shattered when humanity insisted upon its independence and lack of need of God and each other. It is this dependency and vulnerable

---

[62]Copeland, *Enfleshing Freedom*, 104, quoting Bernard Lonergan "The Mystical Body of Christ," *Collected Words of Bernard Lonergan*, vol. 20: *Shorter papers*, ed. Robert C. Croken, Robert M. Doran, and H. Daniel Monsour (Toronto: University of Toronto Press, 2007), 109.

need that is foundational, original, and perfected in the reign of God as absolute interdependency.

An analogy of this interdependent future can be found in the "care webs" described by Leah Lakshmi Piepza-Samarasinha in *Care Work: Dreaming Disability Justice*, elsewhere described as collective care. She writes: "What does it mean to shift our ideas of access and care (whether its disability, childcare, economic access, or many more) from an individual chore, an unfortunate cost of having an unfortunate body, to a collective responsibility that's maybe even deeply joyful?"[63] I quote her example of care webs at length because it helps illustrate what webs of care look like now, in hopes that it can spur our imaginations to think more creatively and hopefully about the kind of vulnerability and communal care that could shape our future eschatological lives together, without the pain behind the requests described, but mirroring the life-giving mutuality and vulnerability that underlies these questions. She begins her essay:

> "Do you have a car today? ...I hurt so bad, can you pick me up? Hey, can I borrow twenty dollars? Can you go buy groceries for me when you're out and drop them off? Here's a list. Do you want to go to community acupuncture today? Hey B. needs more care shifters, can you repost this Facebook note? Can we share the access van ride over to the city? If you come, you can say you're my personal care attendant and you won't have to pay. Do you have anemone tincture you could bring over? I'm flaring. Holding me would be good too. If I take your manual wheelchair and load it up with takeout we'll all have food. Can you go with me to the clinic and take notes while I talk to my doctor? ... Let's pass the hat so we can afford ASL for the event... Here's the list of accessible event spaces we made on Google docs. Can you be part of my mad map crisis fam? Wanna Skype if you can't get out ...?"[64]

Maybe this woven web of lives, vulnerability, and care isn't established in a flash, in a moment of ultimate consummation

---

[63]Leah Lakshmi Piepza-Samarasinha, *Care Work: Dreaming Disability Justice* (Vancouver: Arsenal Pulp Press, 2018), 33.
[64]Piepza-Samarasinha, *Care Work*, 32.

of the eschatological promise, but is deepened and intensified throughout that ongoing journey of body and soul. Maybe like the amputees of Mark, how we enter the resurrected life—as infants or with intellectual impairments or with wheelchairs or histories of survival—isn't a static, unchanging identity. Rather, we become increasingly intertwined, thus more defined by our relationships with God and each other, more transparent in our need, more vulnerable, more eager to meet the needs of another, and ever replenished.

BIBLIOGRAPHY

Althaus-Reid, Marcella. *Indecent Theology: Theological Perversion in Sex, Gender, and Politics* (London: Routledge, 2000).

Althaus-Reid, Marcella. *The Queer God* (New York: Routledge, 2003).

Augustine, Saint. *City of God*, trans. Marcus Dodds, D. D. (New York: Random House, 1993). Modern Library Edition.

Baker Fletcher, Karen. *Dancing with God: The Trinity from a Womanist Perspective* (St. Louis, MO: Chalice Press, 2007).

Barth, Karl. *Church Dogmatics*, 4 volumes in 13 parts, ed. Thomas F. Torrance and Geoffrey W. Bromiley, trans. Geoffrey W. Bromiley (Edinburgh: T&T Clark, 1956–75).

Barth, Karl. "Theological Dialogue," *Theology Today* 19 (2) (July 1962): 171–7.

Barton, Sarah Jean, *Becoming the Baptized Body: Disability and the Practice of Christian Community* (Waco, TX: Baylor University Press, 2022).

Basselin, Timothy. "Why Theology Needs Disability," *Theology Today* 68 (1) (2011): 47–57.

Betcher, Sharon. "Crip/tography: Disability Theology in the Ruins of God," *Journal for Cultural and Religious Theory* 15 (2) (Spring 2016): 98–115.

Betcher, Sharon. "Monstrosities, Miracles, and Mission: Religion and the Politics of Disablement," in *Postcolonial Theologies: Divinity and Empire*, ed. Catherine Keller, Michael Nausner, and Mayra Rivera (St. Louis, MO: Chalice Press, 2004), 79–99.

Betcher, Sharon V. *Spirit and the Politics of Disablement* (Minneapolis: Fortress Press, 2007).

Black, Kathy. *A Healing Homiletic: Preaching and Disability* (Nashville, TN: Abingdon Press, 1996).

The Blessed Theophylact, Archbishop of Ohrid and Bulgaria. "Chapter 2:21–27," in *The Explanation of the Gospel of Luke*, trans. Christopher Stade (House Springs, MO: Chrysostom Press, 1997), 33.

Block, Jennie Weiss. *Copious Hosting: A Theology of Access for Persons with Disabilities* (New York: Continuum, 2002).

Bodley-Dangelo, Faye. *Sexual Difference, Gender, and Agency in Karl Barth's Church Dogmatics* (London: T&T Clark, 2021). E-Book.

Brewer, Elizabeth, and Brenda Jo Brueggemann. "The View from DSQ," *Disability Studies Quarterly* 23 (2) (2014). https://dsq-sds.org/article/view/4258 (accessed October 18, 2022).

Brock, Brian. *Wondrously Wounded: Theology, Disability, and the Body of Christ* (Waco, TX: Baylor University Press, 2019).

Butler, Judith. *Bodies That Matter: On the Discursive Limits of Sex* (London: Routledge, 1993).

Bynum, Caroline Walker. *Fragmentation and Redemption: Essays on Gender and the Human Body in Medieval Religion* (New York: Zone Books, 1992).

Bynum, Caroline Walker. *The Resurrection of the Body in Western Christianity 200–1336* (New York City: Columbia University Press, 1994).

Carter, J. Kameron. *Race: A Theological Account* (Oxford: Oxford University Press, 2008).

Clare, Eli. *Exile and Pride: Disability, Queerness, and Liberation* (Durham: Duke University Press, 2015). Reissue Edition.

Clifton, Shane. *Crippled Grace: Disability, Virtue Ethics, and the Good Life* (Waco, TX: Baylor University Press, 2019).

Coakley, Sarah. *Powers and Submissions: Spirituality, Philosophy, and Gender* (Oxford: Wiley-Blackwell, 2002).

Cone, James H. *God of the Oppressed*, revised edition (Maryknoll, NY: Orbis Press, 1997).

Cone, James H. *The Cross and the Lynching Tree* (Maryknoll, NY: Orbis Books, 2011).

Copeland, M. Shawn. *Enfleshing Freedom: Body, Race, and Being* (Minneapolis, MN: Fortress Press, 2009).

Crawford, Evans E. *The Hum: Call and Response in African American Preaching* (Nashville: Abingdon Press, 1995).

Creamer, Debra. *Disability and Christian Theology: Embodied Limits and Constructive Possibilities* (Oxford: Oxford University Press, 2009).

Creamer, Debra. "Finding God in Our Bodies: Theology from the Perspective of People with Disabilities, Part 2," *Journal of Religion, Disability, and Health*, 2 (2) (1995): 67–87.

Creamer, Debra. "Theological Accessibility: The Contribution of Disability," *Disability Studies Quarterly* 26 (4) (2006). https://dsq-sds.org/article/view/812/987 (accessed October 18, 2022).

Creamer, Debra. "Toward a Theology That Includes the Human Experience of Disability," *Journal of Religion, Disability, and Health* 7 (3) (2003): 57–67.

Daly, Mary. *Beyond God the Father: Toward a Philosophy of Women's Liberation* (Boston: Beacon Press, 1985).

Daniels, Brandy. "Queer Theory," in *Religion: Embodied Religion*, ed. Kent Brintall (New York: Macmillan Reference, 2016), 289–308.

Davis, Lennard. *Enforcing Normalcy: Disability, Deafness, and the Body* (London: Verso, 1995).

Dempsey, Michael T., ed. *Trinity and Election in Contemporary Theology* (Grand Rapids, MI: Eerdmans, 2011).

Eiesland, Nancy. *The Disabled God: Toward a Liberatory Theology of Disability* (Nashville: Abingdon Press, 1994).

Erevelles, Nirmala. "The Color of Violence: Reflecting on Gender, Race, and Disability," in *Feminist Disability Studies*, ed. Kim Q. Hall (Bloomington, IN: Indiana University Press, 2011): 117–35.

Erevelles, Nirmala. *Disability and Difference in Global Contexts: Enabling a Transformative Body Politic* (New York: Palgrave Macmillan, 2011).

Finger, Anne. "Forbidden Fruit," *New Internationalist* (July 5, 1992). https://newint.org/features/1992/07/05/fruit (accessed October 18, 2022).

Freeman, Doreen. "A Feminist Theology of Disability," *Feminist Theology* 10 (29) (2002): 71–85.

Garland-Thomson, Rosemarie. *Extraordinary Bodies: Figuring Disability in American Cultural and Literature* (New York: Columbia University Press, 1996).

Gebara, Ivone. *Longing for Running Water: Ecofeminism and Liberation* (Minneapolis, MN: Fortress, 1999).

Gilbert, Kenyatta R. "The Community's Sage: The Preacher's Call and the Congregation's Response," *Liturgy* 35 (3) (2020): 17–24.

Gonzales, Justo L. *Mañana: Christian Theology from a Hispanic Perspective* (Nashville, Abingdon Press, 1990).

Gould, James Barton. "The Hope of Heavenly Healing of Disability Part 1: Theological Issues," *Journal of Disability & Religion*, 20 (4) (2016): 317–34.

Gould, James Barton. "The Hope of Heavenly Healing of Disability Part 2—Philosophical Issues," *Journal of Disability & Religion*, 21 (1) (2017): 98–116.

Gregory of Nyssa. *Commentary on the Song of Songs*, trans. Casimir McCambley. (Brookline, MA: Hellenic College Press, 1987).

Gregory of Nyssa. *The Life of Saint Macrina*, trans. Kevin Corrigan (Eugene, OR: Wipt & Stock, 2001).

Hampson, Daphne, ed. *Swallowing a Fishbone? Feminist Theologians Debate Christology* (London: SPCK, 1996).

Harrison, Robert D., and Linda K. Harrison. "The Call from the Mountaintop: Call-Response and the Oratory of Martin Luther King, Jr.," in *Martin Luther King, Jr. and the Sermonic Power of Public Discourse*, ed. Carolyn Calloway-Thomas and John Louis Lucaites (Tuscaloosa: University of Alabama Press, 1993), 162–78.

Hauerwas, Stanley. "Suffering the Retarded: Should We Prevent Retardation?," in *Critical Reflections on Stanley Hauerwas' Theology of Disability: Disabling Society, Enabling Theology*, ed. John Swinton (Binghamton, NY: Haworth Pastoral Press, 2004), 87–106.

Hector, Kevin W. "God's Triunity and Self-Determination: A Conversation with Karl Barth, Bruce McCormack, and Paul Molnar," in *Trinity and Election in Contemporary Theology*, ed. Michael T. Dempsey (Grand Rapids, MI: Eerdmans, 2011), 29–46.

Henderson-Espinoza, Robyn. *Body Becoming: A Path to Our Liberation* (Minneapolis, MN: Broadleaf Books, 2022).

Henderson-Espinoza, Robyn. "Decolonial Erotics: Power Bottoms, Topping from Bottom Space, and the Emergence of a Queer Sexual Theology," *Feminist Theology* 26 (3) (2018): 286–96.

Henderson-Espinoza, Robyn. "Difference, Becoming, and Interrelatedness: A Material Resistance Becoming," *CrossCurrents* (June 2016): 281–9.

Henderson-Espinoza, Robyn. "Transing Religion: Moving Beyond the Logic of the (Hetero)Norm of Binaries," *Journal of Feminist Studies in Religion* 34 (1): 88–92.

Hollywood, Amy. "That Glorious Slit: Irigaray and the Medieval Devotion to Christ's Side Wound," in *Luce Irigaray and Premodern Culture*, ed. Elizabeth Harvey and Theresa Krier (London: Routledge, 2004), 120.

Jenson, Robert. "Once More the *Logos Asarkos*," *International Journal of Systematic Theology* 13 (1) (2011): 130–3.

Johnson, Elizabeth. *She Who Is: The Mystery of God in Feminist Discourse* (New York: Crossroads, 1992).

Johnson, Elizabeth. *Quest for the Living God: Mapping Frontiers in the Theology of God* (New York: Continuum, 2007).

Jones, Paul Dafydd. *The Humanity of Christ: Christology in Karl Barth's Church Dogmatics* (New York: T&T Clark, 2011).

Jowers, Dennis W., and H. Wayne House, eds. *The New Evangelical Subordinationism?: Perspectives on the Equality of God the Father and God the Son* (Eugene, OR: Pickwick, 2012).

Jüngel, Eberhard. *God's Being Is in His Becoming: The Trinitarian Being of God in the Theology of Karl Barth*, trans. John Webster (London: T&T Clark, 2014).

Kafer, Alison. "Un/Safe Disclosures: Scenes of Disability and Trauma," *Journal of Literary and Cultural Disability Studies* 10 (1) (2016): 1–20.

Kafer, Alison. *Feminist, Queer, Crip* (Bloomington: University of Indiana Press, 2013).

Keller, Katherine. *Face of the Deep: A Theology of Becoming* (New York: Routledge, 2003).

Kittay, Eva. *Learning from My Daughter: The Value and Care of Disabled Minds* (Oxford: Oxford University Press, 2019).

Kittay, Eva. *Loves Labor: Essays on Women, Equality, and Dependency* (New York: Routledge, 1999).

Marcus, Joel. *Mark 8–16*, Anchor Yale Bible Commentary (New Haven, CT: Yale University Press, 2009), 690.

Martin, Emily. "The Egg and the Sperm: How Science Has Constructed a Romance Based on Stereotypical Male-Female Roles," *Signs* 16 (3) (1991): 485–501.

McCormack, Bruce L. "The Actuality of God: Karl Barth in Conversation with Open Theism," in *Engaging the Doctrine of God: Contemporary Protestant Perspectives* (Grand Rapids, MI: Baker Academic, 2008), 185–244.

McCormack, Bruce L. "Divine Impassibility or Simply Divine Constancy?: Implications of Karl Barth's Later Christology for Debates over Impassibility," *Divine Impassibility and the Mystery of Human Suffering* (2009): 150–86.

McCormack, Bruce L. "Election and Trinity: Thesis in Response to George Hunsinger," in *Trinity and Election in Contemporary Theology*, ed. Michael T. Dempsey (Grand Rapids, MI: Eerdmans, 2011), 115–37.

McCormack, Bruce L. "Grace and Being: The Role of God's Gracious Election in Karl Barth's Theological Ontology," in *The Cambridge Companion to Karl Barth*, ed. John Webster (Cambridge: Cambridge University Press, 2000), 92–110.

McCormack, Bruce L. *The Humility of the Eternal Son: Reformed Kenoticism and the Repair of Chalcedon* (Cambridge: Cambridge University Press, 2021).

McCormack, Bruce L. "The Identity of the Son: Karl Barth's Exegesis of Hebrews 1.1–4 (And Similar Passages)," in *Christology, Hermeneutics, and Hebrews: Profiles from the History of Interpretation*, ed. Jon C. Laansma and Daniel L. Treier (New York: T&T Clark, 2012), 155–72.

McCormack, Bruce, L. *Orthodox and Modern: Studies in the Theology of Karl Barth* (Grand Rapids, MI: Baker Academic, 2008).

McCormack, Bruce L. "Kenoticism in Modern Christology," in *The Oxford Handbook of Christology*, ed. Francesca Aran Murphy (Oxford: Oxford University Press, 2015), 444–60.

McCormack, Bruce L. "The Lord and Giver of Life: A Barthian Defense of the Filioque," in *Rethinking Trinitarian Theology: Disputed Questions and Contemporary Issues in Trinitarian Theology*, ed. Guilio Maspero and Robert Wozniak (New York: T&T Clark, 2012), 230–53.

McCormack, Bruce L. "The Person of Christ," in *Mapping Modern Theology: A Thematic and Historical Introduction*, ed. Kelly M. Kapic and Bruce L. McCormack (Grand Rapids, MI: Baker Academic, 2012), 149–74.

McCormack, Bruce L. "Processions and Missions: A Point of Convergence between Thomas Aquinas and Karl Barth," in *Thomas Aquinas and Karl Barth: An Unofficial Catholic-Protestant Dialogue*, ed. Bruce L. McCormack and Thomas Joseph White (Grand Rapids, MI: Eerdmans, 2013), 99–128.

McCormack, Bruce L. "Seek God Where He May Be Found: A Response to Edwin van Driel," *Scottish Journal of Theology* 60 (1) (2007): 62–79.

McFague, Sallie. *The Body of God: An Ecological Theology* (Minneapolis, MN: Fortress Press, 1993).

McKelway, Alexander J. "Perichoretic Possibilities in Barth's Doctrine of Male and Female," *Princeton Seminary Bulletin* 7 (3) (1986): 231–43.

McRuer, Robert. *Crip Theory: Cultural Signs of Queerness and Disability* (New York: New York University Press, 2006).

Mercedes, Anna. *Power For: Feminism and Christ's Self-Giving* (New York City: T&T Clark, 2011).

Mingus, Mia. "Changing the Framework: Disability Justice—How Our Communities Can Move beyond Access to Wholeness." https://leavinge vidence.wordpress.com/2011/02/12/changing-the-framework-disabil ity-justice/ (accessed October 18, 2022).

Mingus, Mia. "Moving toward the Ugly: A Politic beyond Desirability." https://leavingevidence.wordpress.com/2011/08/22/moving-tow ard-the-ugly-a-politic-beyond-desirability/ (accessed October 18, 2022).

Mingus, Mia. Interview by ALOK for *Them* Magazine. https://www.them. us/story/ugliness-disability-mia-mingus (accessed October 18, 2022).

Molnar, Paul. *Divine Freedom and the Doctrine of the Immanent Trinity: In Dialogue with Karl Barth and Contemporary Theology*, 2nd edition (London: T&T Clark, 2017).

Molnar, Paul. *Faith, Freedom, and the Spirit: The Economic Trinity in Barth, Torrence, and Contemporary Theology* (Downers Grove, IL: InterVarsity Press, 2015).

Moss, Candida. *Divine Bodies: Resurrecting Perfection in the New Testament and Early Christianity* (New Haven, CT: Yale University Press, 2019).

Moore, Stephen D., Kent Brintnall, and Joseph Marchall. "Queer Disorientations: Four Turns and a Twist," in *Sexual Disorientations: Queer Temporalities, Affects, Theologies*, ed. Kent Brintnall, Joseph Marchall, and Stephen D. Moore (New York: Fordam University Press, 2018), 14.

Mullins, R. T. "Some Difficulties for Amos Yong's Disability Theology of the Resurrection," *Ars Disputandi* 11 (1) (2011): 24–32.

Muñoz, Esteban José. *Cruising Utopia: The Then and There of Queer Futurity* (New York: New York University Press, 2009), 32.

Pârvan, Alexandra, and Bruce L. McCormack. "Immutability, (Im)possibility, and Suffering: Steps toward a 'Psychological' Ontology of God," *Neue Zeitschrift für Systematische Theologie und Relgionsphilosophie* 59 (1) (2017): 1–25.

Piepza-Samarasinha, Leah Lakshmi. *Care Work: Dreaming Disability Justice* (Vancouver: Arsenal Pulp Press, 2018).

Powell, Lisa D. "Disability and Resurrection: Eschatological Bodies, Identity, and Continuity," *Journal of the Society of Christian Ethics* 41 (1) (Spring/Summer 2021): 89–106.

Powell, Lisa D. "Disability and Covenant Ontology," in *Karl Barth and Liberation Theology*, ed. Kaitlyn Dugan and Paul Dafydd Jones (London: T&T Clark, 2023): 69–84.

Powell, Lisa D. "The Infertile Womb of God: Ableism in Feminist Doctrine of God," *CrossCurrents* 65 (1) (March 2015): 116–38.

Powell, Lisa D. "Resurrection and Queer Identity," in *Routledge Companion to Christian Ethics*, ed. D. Stephen Long and Rebekah L. Miles (London: Routledge, 2023), 275–88.

Puar, Jasbir K. *The Right to Maim: Debility, Capacity, and Disability* (Durham, NC: Duke University Press, 2017).

Quick, Laura. "Bitenosh's Orgasm, Galen's Two Seeds and Conception Theory in the Hebrew Bible," *Dead Sea Discoveries* 28 (2021): 38–63.

Raffety, Erin. *From Inclusion to Justice: Disability, Ministry, and Congregational Leadership* (Waco, TX: Baylor University Press, 2022).

Rivera, Mayra. *The Touch of Transcendence: A Postcolonial Theology of God* (Louisville, KY: Westminster John Knox Press, 2007).

Reinders, Hans S. *Receiving the Gift of Friendship: Profound Disability, Theological Anthropology, and Ethics* (Grand Rapids, MI: Eerdmans, 2008).

Reuther, Rosemary Radford. *Sexism and Godtalk: Toward a Feminist Theology* (Boston, MA: Beacon Press, 1993).

Reynolds, Thomas E. *Vulnerable Communion: Theology of Disability and Hospitality* (Grand Rapids, MI: Brazos Press, 2008).

Sandahl, Carrie. "Queering Crip or Cripping the Queer?: Intersections of Queer and Crip Identities in Solo Autobiographical Performance," in *A Journal of Gay and Lesbian Studies* 9 (1–2) (2003): 25–56.

Schipper, Jeremy. *Disability and Isaiah's Suffering Servant* (Oxford: Oxford University Press, 2011).

Schneiders, Sandra. *Women and the Word: The Gender of God in the New Testament and the Spirituality of Women* (New York: Paulist Press, 1986).

Seibers, Tobin. "A Sexual Culture for People with Disabilities," in *Sex and Disability*, ed. Robert McRuer and Anna Mollow (Durham, NC: Duke University Press, 2012), 37–53.

Shakespeare, Tom. "Disabled Sexuality: Toward Rights and Recognition," *Sexuality and Disability* 18 (3) (2000): 59–66.

Smith, Aaron T. "God's Self-Specification: His Being Is His Electing," in *Trinity and Election in Contemporary Theology*, ed. Michael T. Dempsey (Grand Rapids, MI: Eerdmans, 2011), 201–28.

Soldatic, Karen, and Shaun Grech. "Transnationalising Disability Studies: Rights, Justice, and Impairment," *Disability Studies Quarterly* 34 (2) (2014). https://dsq-sds.org/article/view/4249 (accessed October 18, 2022).

Spies, Miriam. "Liturgical Imagination at Full Stretch: Possibilities for Leadership of Disabled People," *Concilium* 5 (2020): 128–37.

Spies, Miriam. "Making Space, Offering Voice: Leadership of People with Disabilities in God's Mission," *International Review of Missions* 108 (1) (June 2019): 25–37.

Springs, Jason A. "Following at a Distance (Again): Gender, Equality, and Freedom in Karl Barth," *Modern Theology* 28 (3) (July 2012): 446–77.

Stephenson, Lisa P. "Directed, Ordered and Related: The Male and Female Interpersonal Relation in Karl Barth's Church Dogmatics," *Scottish Journal of Theology* 61 (4) (2008): 435–49.

Sumner, Darren O. *Karl Barth and the Incarnation: Christology and the Humility of God* (New York: T&T Clark, 2016).

Swinton, John. "Who Is the God We Worship? Theologies of Disability; Challenges and New Possibilities," *International Journal of Practical Theology* 14 (2) (2011): 273–307.

Tataryn, Myroslaw, and Maria Truchan-Tataryn. *Discovering Trinity in Disability: A Theology for Embracing Difference* (Maryknoll, NY: Orbis Books, 2013).

Thatcher, Adrian. *Gender and Christian Ethics* (Cambridge: Cambridge University Press, 2021).

Tonstad, Linn Marie. *God and Difference: The Trinity, Sexuality, and the Transformation of Finitude* (New York: Routledge Press, 2016).

Tonstad, Linn Marie. "The Logic of Origin and the Paradoxes of Language: A Theological Experiment," *Modern Theology* 30 (3) (July 2014): 50–73.

Tran, Jonathan. *Asian Americans and the Spirit of Racial Capitalism* (Oxford: Oxford University Press, 2022).

Ward, Graham. "Bodies: The Displaced Body of Jesus Christ," in *Radical Orthodoxy: A New Theology*, ed. John Milbank, Catherine Pickstock, and Graham Ward (London: Routledge, 1999), 163–81.

Ward, Graham. *Christ and Culture* (London: Blackwell Publishing, 2005).

Ward, Graham. "There Is no Sexual Difference," in *Queer Theology: Rethinking the Western Body* (Oxford: Blackwell Publishing, 2007), 76–85.

Wendell, Susan. *The Rejected Body: Feminist Philosophical Reflections on Disability* (New York: Routledge, 1996).

Wilkerson, Abby. "Disability, Sex Radicalism, and Political Agency," in *Feminist Disability Studies*, ed. Kim Q. Hall (Bloomington: Indiana University Press, 2011): 193–217.

Yong, Amos. "Disability Theology of the Resurrection: Persisting Questions and Additional Considerations—A Response to Ryan Mullins," *Ars Disputandi* 12 (1) (2012): 4–10.

Yong, Amos. *Theology and Down Syndrome: Reimagining Disability in Late Modernity* (Waco, TX: Baylor University Press, 2007).

INDEX